Learning CAD with
AutoS

CW01558842

Other Titles of Interest

Learning CAD with AutoSketch for Windows

by

J. W. PENFOLD

BERNARD BABANI (publishing) LTD
THE GRAMPIANS
SHEPHERDS BUSH ROAD
LONDON W6 7NF
ENGLAND

PLEASE NOTE

Although every care has been taken with the production of this book to ensure that any projects, designs, modifications and/or programs, etc., contained herewith, operate in a correct and safe manner and also that any components specified are normally available in Great Britain, the Publishers and Author(s) do not accept responsibility in any way for the failure (including fault in design) of any project, design, modification or program to work correctly or to cause damage to any equipment that it may be connected to or used in conjunction with, or in respect of any other damage or injury that may be so caused, nor do the Publishers accept responsibility in any way for the failure to obtain specified components.

Notice is also given that if equipment that is still under warranty is modified in any way or used or connected with home-built equipment then that warranty may be void.

First Published - April 1994

British Library Cataloguing in Publication Data:
Penfold, J. W.
    Learning CAD with AutoSketch for Windows
    I. Title
    006.6

    ISBN 0 85934 250 6

Printed and Bound in Great Britain by Cox & Wyman Ltd, Reading

PREFACE

This book serves two purposes. Firstly, it is a book for AutoSketch users. Secondly, it is a general introduction to the subject of Computer Aided Drawing (CAD). These two go easily together, because AutoSketch is a low-cost but remarkably comprehensive CAD program. It is ideal for learning the basics, though certainly capable of being used for real applications.

AutoSketch has nearly all the features found in more expensive CAD programs, though, as might be expected, the implementation of these features may be less comprehensive. Once you have learned to use AutoSketch, should your needs outgrow it, you will be well placed to move on to the more advanced programs. Many people will, however, find AutoSketch fully capable of fulfilling their needs.

CAD has a very wide range of applications. The fact that AutoSketch comes with fonts of mapping, mathematical and music symbols is evidence of this. CAD can touch almost any business, profession, craft or pastime which uses drawings (try to think of one that doesn't!). It is hoped this book will help and encourage you to explore at least part of this scope.

This book is applicable to both Release 1 and Release 2 of AutoSketch for Windows.

J. W. Penfold.

The Author wishes to thank his brother R. A. Penfold for the use of the electronic circuit in Figure 4.4. This comes from BP 321, 'Circuit Source - Book 1', Page 15.

TRADEMARKS

CONTENTS

1. FINDING YOUR WAY

This book is about learning Computer Aided Design (CAD) in general, and about learning to use AutoSketch for Windows in particular. Despite its name, AutoSketch is definitely a CAD program, though its uses extend to graphics and DTP. If you have previously used 'paint' type computer graphics programs (for example, the Microsoft Paintbrush program which is provided with Microsoft Windows, or De Luxe Paint 2 from Electronic Arts), you will find AutoSketch very different.

The Screen
When you start AutoSketch, you are presented with a screen divided into several parts (see Figure 1.1).

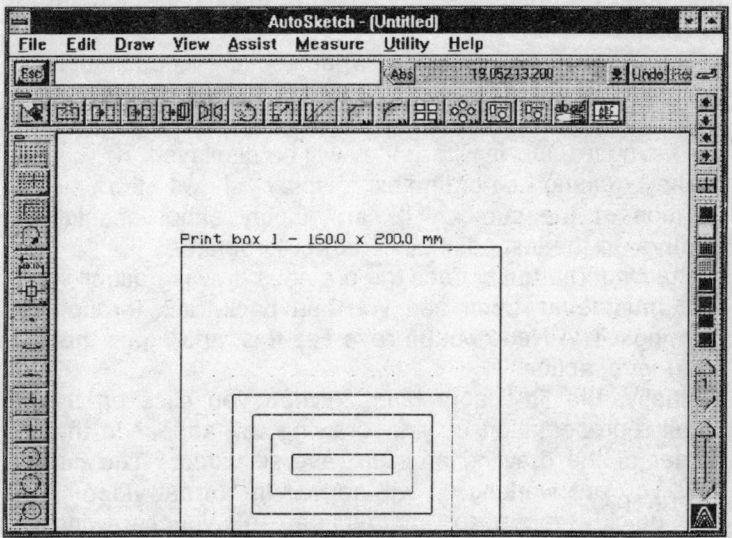

Figure 1.1.   The AutoSketch screen.

The top of the screen carries the caption bar. This is typical of Windows programs, but in AutoSketch, it will change to indicate the tool in use or the operation being carried out.

1

Below this comes the Menu Bar, a feature now very common in computing. Menus can pop down from this in conventional fashion, but most of the menus can also display as toolboxes. These appear between the menu bar and the drawing area. Users of previous versions of AutoSketch will note that the menus now follow Windows (and CUA) conventions, in that File is now the leftmost menu, and the old Change menu is now Edit.

It is only the File and Help menus (another new feature) which must display as menus. All the rest can be displayed as toolboxes.

Next line down is the Prompt line. From left to right, this carries an Escape button, the prompt box, the running co-ordinates display, the Undo and Redo buttons, and finally a little aeroplane.

The Escape button allows you to abandon the current operation. It duplicates the action of the Escape key on the keyboard.

The Prompt box tells you what you are supposed to do next, for example, select a point or select an object, depending on the operation. If you enter co-ordinates from the keyboard, this is where they will be displayed.

The running co-ordinates display shows the current position of the cursor. It can display either absolute or relative (to the last point selected) co-ordinates.

The Undo button undoes the previous drawing action. This is a multi-level undo, and you can back-track through the drawing. The Redo button reverses this, and again this is a multi-level action.

Finally, the little aeroplane. When you click on this, a small representation of your drawing will appear in the top corner of the drawing area, in reverse video. The current area you are working on will appear in normal video. You can quickly move to another part of your drawing by dragging this area.

Next down comes the Toolbox area. This displays the currently selected toolbox. In the screen in Figure 1.1, the Edit toolbox is shown.

Normally, the Assist toolbox is shown down the left side of the screen, but this can be changed or removed if required.

Down the right of the screen, from top to bottom, are the scroll buttons, for moving around the drawing area, colour selection boxes, the layer selector, line style selector, and at the bottom, the AutoDesk logo. Clicking on this redraws the screen.

The area between these is the actual drawing surface. You can display the whole of your drawing, or any selected part, in this area. AutoSketch uses an arrow pointer, which will initially be seen in the middle of this area.

With a mouse, AutoSketch uses only the left button, the usual select or pick button. This is not standard among CAD programs, some of which require a three-button mouse and use all three buttons. On a graphics tablet, it will normally be the point button which is used, but this may vary, depending on the actual graphics tablet and the driver used. In some cases, any button will work.

If you are using keyboard control, the cursor 'arrow' keys move the pointer, and the Ins key (normally used to toggle between insert and overwrite modes in text programs) is used as the button. Use of the keyboard is slow, and can be irksome for extended use. It is possible to draw without using the pointer, by entering drawing commands and co-ordinates on the prompt line. This drawing method sounds like awfully hard work, but in fact it has its uses, and is certainly easier than moving the pointer with the keyboard.

Command Outlines

This section briefly lists all the AutoSketch commands on a menu-by-menu basis. The information here is intended to give an overview of AutoSketch, and is a description of the capabilities rather than working instructions. More information on how to use the commands, with examples, is given in the following chapters.

File Menu

This menu has all the commands to do with saving and loading files, including saving drawings, or selected parts of drawings, as 'parts' which can be used as standard components in future drawings. It also has the commands to print or plot a drawing.

New is used to start a new drawing. If your current drawing has been altered since it was last saved, you will be asked if you want to save it. The screen is then cleared in readiness for starting the new drawing. Units and other settings are not reset to defaults.

Open reloads an existing file for further work, for review or for printing. A dialogue box is produced, from which you can select the file to be opened. If you have chosen to display files as icons, the default, the dialog will display a small representation of each available drawing. The dialog is shown in Figure 1.2.

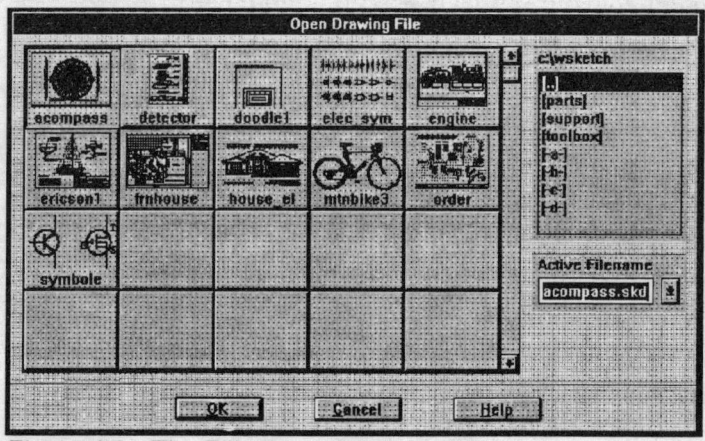

Figure 1.2. The File Open dialog.

Save saves the current drawing using its current filename. If you have never saved your drawing, this command is the same as Save As. Save should be used periodically when working on a drawing as a precaution against power cuts or similar hiatuses. It is a good idea to save immediately after completing any particularly difficult parts!

Save As allows a file to be saved under a new filename. The file under the old name is left unchanged on the disk. This command can be used when saving a drawing for the first time (though in this instance Save will also prompt for a filename), or to allow a file to be modified whilst preserving the original. If you intend doing this, it is a good idea to use

Save As immediately after loading the file. This will avoid accidentally changing the disk file by choosing Save by mistake. If you have a file which will often be used in this way, as a starting point for future drawings, it can be protected from inadvertent modification by making it read-only with the DOS ATTRIB command.

Part Clip allows the whole or selected objects from the current drawing to be saved as a part file. This can subsequently be selected with the Part command on the DRAW menu, and inserted into the original or any other drawing. Note that there is no distinction between a part and a drawing in AutoSketch. Any drawing can be used as a part. Chapter 3 covers this subject in detail. Equally, any part can be considered a complete drawing, so this command could be used to extract parts of a drawing to be used independently.

Import DXF allows a DXF file, from AutoSketch or another program which supports this format, to be read in. There are limitations on what AutoSketch can read in, however.

Export DXF is used to save the current drawing as an AutoCAD DXF format file. This can be read in by AutoCAD release 9 or higher, and can also be read by some other programs, such as DTP.

View Slide is the counterpart of Export Slide, and is used to display slide images on the screen.

Export Slide is used to make a copy of the current screen image to a file. Slide files can be loaded and displayed much quicker than drawing files when reviewing drawings, but the view cannot be altered in any way, and no work can be done on a drawing loaded as a slide. It is strictly a copy of the screen image. Some Desktop Publishing (DTP) programs can read in .SLD files, but as these are saved at screen resolution, the quality is usually unacceptable for serious work.

Quit exits AutoSketch. If the drawing has been modified since it was last saved, you will be prompted to save it if you wish to do so.

Edit Menu

The items on the Edit menu are used to alter parts of an existing drawing. The item or items to be changed must be selected by using the hand pointer, which will appear when you make a selection from this menu. To select more than one item, point to an empty area of the screen. You will then be prompted to enter the corner of a crosses box or a window box. The differences between these are the way in which they are drawn and the way in which they select objects.

If you start at a point to the left of the objects you wish to include, and pick the second corner to the right, a solid box will be drawn. This is a window box, and only objects which lie entirely within the box area will be selected. Objects partially within the box will not be selected.

If you start at a point to the right of the objects you wish to include, and pick the second corner to the left, a dotted box will be drawn. This is a crosses box, and any objects wholly or partially within this box will be selected.

There are special rules concerning how some objects are selected. Some commands allow multiple objects to be selected one at a time. Others only allow use of a box. These will be described in later chapters.

Break can be used to trim the ends off objects, or to cut an object in two by removing a part from the middle. You can Break arcs, boxes, circles, lines, polygons, and curve frames, but you cannot use this command on grouped objects. The keyboard equivalent is F4.

Copy is used to make duplicates of objects within a drawing. It is essentially similar to Move, except that the object (or objects) is (are) left at their original location. The keyboard equivalent is F6.

Erase is used to erase selected objects from the drawing, both from the screen and from memory. The keyboard equivalent is F3.

Mirror creates mirror images of existing objects. You must select the objects to be mirrored. and then the two points describing the line about which the objects will be mirrored. The keyboard equivalent is Ctrl + F3.

6

Move is used to move objects from place to place in a drawing. You must provide two points. The first is a base point on the object (or relative to the objects) to be moved. The second is the insertion point. The base point is moved to the insertion point. The keyboard equivalent is F5.

Multiple Copy is similar to Copy, but it allows many copies of the selected objects to be made, without repeatedly having to reselect them.

Property is used to change the colour, layer, dimension units, line type and text to the current values.

Rotate is used to rotate objects. This can be done with the pointer, but is one command where it is often much more useful to enter the rotation angle from the keyboard. The Ortho and Snap commands will affect the way Rotate works. The keyboard equivalent is Ctrl + F5.

Scale is used to alter the size of objects in a drawing. Fortunately, unlike some previous versions of AutoSketch, the scaling factor to be used can now be typed in. Scaling was one of the most difficult operations in early releases. It is now quite easy and straightforward. The keyboard equivalent is Ctrl + F6.

Stretch is used to stretch objects in a drawing. Most objects can be stretched, including text. Circles cannot be stretched, as this would distort them. Circles may be moved by the stretch command if the centre point is selected, otherwise they are unaffected. The same applies to ellipses. There are other restrictions on this command. The keyboard equivalent is F7.

Text Editor is essentially the same as on the Draw menu. It is included here as it is used to modify existing text as well as to create new text items. It is shown in Figure 1.3.

Chamfer is used to trim two lines which intersect, and connect the ends with a new line. The two lines do not need to meet to use this command. AutoSketch will extend them if necessary. This command cannot be used on boxes or polygons unless you convert them to line segments. It cannot work on parallel lines.

Fillet is similar to Chamfer, except that it joins the trimmed lines with a curved fillet instead of a straight line. The same restrictions apply. You must select the two lines, and also the fillet radius, which must not be too large.

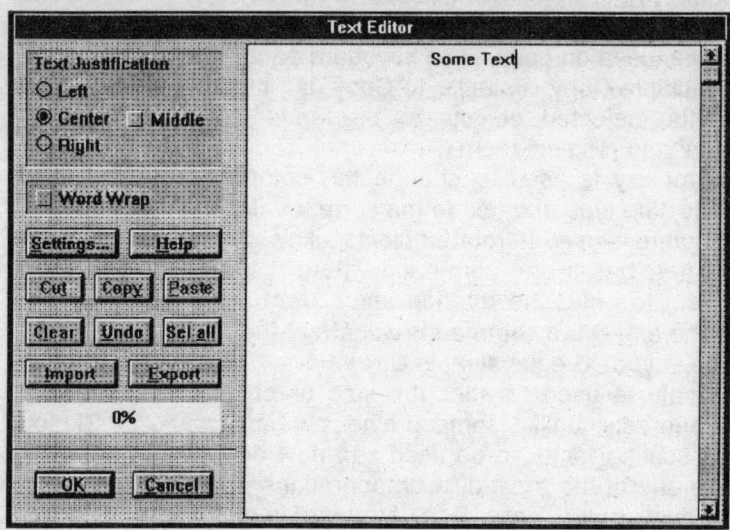

Figure 1.3. The Text Editor.

Box Array is used to make multiple copies of an object in a pattern of rows and columns. The number of rows and columns, and the baseline angle, can be set. The spacings can also be set, or the array can be made to fit in a given space. The keyboard equivalent is Ctrl + F2.

Ring Array makes multiple copies of an object in a circular pattern. The number of items must be set, and you can also set either the angle between them or the total angle to fill, in which case the angle is calculated for you. You must also select the centre point for the array, and the distance between this and the original object gives the radius of the array. The object may optionally be rotated as it is copied. The keyboard equivalent is Ctrl + F4.

Group is used to group a set of single objects together, so that they can be treated as a single object. This command operates hierarchically. This means that objects within a group can themselves be grouped objects. Grouping objects is very useful if they are to be copied or moved within a drawing, or saved as a part for use in other drawings. It prevents component objects from being 'left behind'. The keyboard equivalent is Alt + F9.

Ungroup is used to 'explode' a grouped object, so that its component parts may be treated as separate entities again. Like group, it works hierarchically. It must be used more than once to fully explode 'groups of groups'. The keyboard equivalent is Alt + F10.

Draw Menu

This menu has all the commands for actually drawing. It will probably be the one used most in the execution of a drawing. It will normally always be best to display this as a toolbox (the default). It is then possible to change properties (where appropriate) by double-clicking on the toolbox buttons. Otherwise, you have to go via the Drawing Settings item on the Utility menu.

Arc draws a portion of a circle. You must specify the two endpoints, and a position on the arc. AutoSketch calculates the radius from these three points. The keyboard equivalent is Alt + F3 (i.e. hold down the Alt key and press F3 briefly).

Box draws a rectangular box. You must specify two diagonally opposite corners. The keyboard equivalent is Ctrl + F4.

Circle draws a circle. You must specify the centre point, and a point on the circle. As usual in CAD programs, circles cannot be stretched into ellipses. The keyboard equivalent is Alt + F4.

Curve draws a B-spline curve. Curves can be closed or open. You must specify a starting point, a variable number of control points, and an end point (by selecting the same point twice, or reselecting the start point for a closed curve).

Ellipse is used to draw ellipses. Three methods of drawing ellipses are provided. The axes of ellipses do not need to be aligned with the x- and y-axes of the drawing, and any aspect ratio can be obtained. The keyboard equivalent is Ctrl +F8.

Line is used to draw single lines. You must specify a start point and an end point. A series of connected lines can be drawn by selecting the end point of one as the start point of the next. However, these will be treated as separate entities. The keyboard equivalent is Alt + F1.

Pattern Fill is used to create areas which are filled with patterns. This is the only way in which areas may be filled with patterns. It is not possible to fill other objects, or areas between objects. Various fill patterns may be used (including a solid fill and 'blank' fill). AutoSketch comes with a collection of fill pattern files, and user-defined fills can also be created. The outline of the area to be filled consists of zero-width polylines, which may be invisible, and the boundary may include arc sections (but not spline curves) as well as straight lines. The keyboard equivalent is Ctrl + F9.

Point is used to draw a dot at a specified location. They can be used to align and attach other objects, but do not print or plot.

Polyline is used to draw a series of connected lines and arc sections. A polyline can have a defined width and, optionally, a fill pattern (for the lines, not the area they enclose). A polyline with a defined width is different to a normal line, which has a theoretical zero width, and is rendered as one pixel wide on the output device. Polylines can also have 'zero width', in which case they are also drawn one pixel wide. As normal lines can be difficult to see if printed on a high-resolution printer (e.g. a laser printer), you may find you need to use polylines a good deal. Polylines can be used to draw open or closed figures. The keyboard equivalent is Alt + F2.

Quick Text is used to draw text. Size, font, under/overlining, and other effects, can be selected. Quick Text can have left, right or centre justification from a chosen point. It is used for adding small amounts of text, such as labels and captions.

Text Editor is used for adding substantial amounts of text. It allows all normal text editing features, such as insert, delete, cut, copy and paste. This feature can also import text from other programs, and export text, as well as creating text in a drawing. It is useful for cases where a drawing will include a lot of text, such as presentation material, or for importing standard text, such as disclaimers or copyright notices.

Part is not exactly a drawing command. It is used to insert a previously saved AutoSketch drawing in a new drawing. Libraries of re-usable components can be created. Parts do not have to be saved in a special format. When this command is chosen, you are presented with a dialog from which the part can be chosen. Parts are displayed as icons in buttons. This is shown in Figure 1.4.

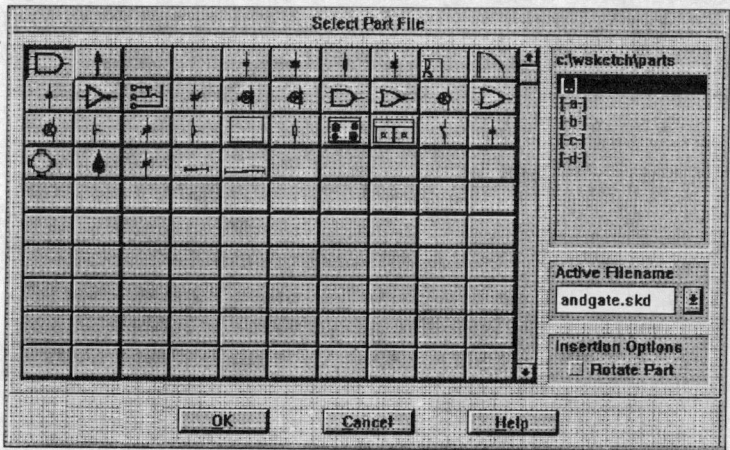

Figure 1.4. The Select Part dialog.

View Menu

This menu allows you to move around your drawing and to display it at a larger or smaller scale. None of the items on this menu actually change the drawing.

An alternative to this is provided by the Aerial view feature, which shows a small version of the drawing, with the current area highlighted. You can pan around the drawing by 'dragging' this highlighted area.

Last Print Box fills the screen with the drawing to the extents of the last plot box you created during the current drawing session. Print boxes are used to position the drawing on the page before printing, and are explained further later in this book.

Last View allows you to return to where you were before using any of the other commands on this menu (except

11

redraw). It could be thought of as a View Undo. You can also use this command to toggle between two views, perhaps two places on the drawing, or two different scales. The keyboard equivalent is F9.

Zoom Box allows you to select an area on the screen by drawing a box around the area of current interest. This area is zoomed to fill the whole screen. You draw the box by selecting two diagonally opposite corners, and it makes no difference whether you draw it to the right or left. This command is very useful for large changes in scale. The keyboard equivalent is F10.

Zoom Full resizes the drawing so that all the objects are shown, at as large a scale as possible. The area displayed may be only part of the drawing limits, or may extend beyond them.

Zoom Limits resizes the drawing on the screen so that all of the drawing out to the drawing limits is included. The drawing limits are set from Drawing Settings (Limits/Grid/Snap) on the Utility menu.

Zoom X allows you to change the size of the displayed drawing using a scale factor, entered from the keyboard. You can use values of between 0 and 1 to shrink the drawing (and display more of it) or greater than 1 to enlarge it.

Redraw forces a full screen redraw. This can be useful if you have been doing a lot of editing, and many lines in the drawing have breaks in them as a result. It will also restore missing dots in the grid. A quicker alternative is to click on the AutoDesk trademark button on the lower right of the screen.

Pan is used to alter the part of the drawing displayed, without altering the scale. You must pick a reference point on the drawing, and then a point on the screen. The reference point will be shifted to the point on the screen. This command is affected by Ortho and Snap. You may use the Scroll buttons instead of this command. They are perhaps easier to use (this method is somewhat counter-intuitive), but this command can be quicker. The keyboard equivalent of Pan is F8.

Fill is a toggle. When it is on, fill patterns are displayed on the screen. When it is off, they are not. Turning fill off speeds redrawing.

Text is another toggle. When it is on, text is displayed as text. When it is off, boxes are drawn around areas text will occupy. Again, this speeds redrawing.

Frame is the third toggle in this group. When it is on, frames are drawn around curves. These are used in editing curves. When off, only the frames are drawn.

Assist Menu

The items on this menu are switches which can be on or off. They control drawing aids, which assist in accuracy and alignment. If a tick (check mark) appears beside an item on this menu, it is 'on', or currently active. Otherwise, it is 'off', or inactive.

The items on this menu are so useful that they are normally also displayed in a toolbox to the left of the screen, so they are instantly available. Some of them need to be available quickly, as they may be turned on or off in the middle of a drawing operation. When on, the toolbar buttons will appear depressed, and will also show a dotted outline around the button graphic.

Grid displays a rectangular grid of points (dots) on the screen. The spacings between the dots is user-selectable. You can use these to help you accurately place objects in your drawing, and make the relative size of objects correct. Turning the grid on does not force the cursor to points on the grid. The Snap setting does this. The Grid setting is independent of the Snap setting, but if you set the Grid spacing to zero, the Snap setting is used. The keyboard equivalent is Alt + F6.

Snap restricts point selection to predetermined regularly spaced points. When Snap is on, the pointer can be placed between these points, but a cursor (a small cross) will jump from one to the next. Only cursor positions can be selected. This is used to enforce accurate placement of objects. The Snap points are not displayed, but the Grid and Snap settings can be made the same by setting the Grid spacing to zero. With both Grid and Snap, the vertical and horizontal spacings may be different. The keyboard equivalent is Alt + F7.

Ortho restricts drawn lines, and some other commands, to exact vertical and horizontal directions only. When Ortho is on, rotation can only work in 90 degree steps, and Mirror and Pan are also affected. The keyboard equivalent is Alt + F5.

Arc Mode determines whether the Polyline or Pattern Fill functions on the Draw menu draw line segments or arcs. When it is on, arcs are drawn, and when off, line segments are drawn. This command is one which will be turned on and off while drawing. The keyboard equivalent is Ctrl + F1.

Attach is used to accurately attach new objects to existing ones. When you select a point when Attach is on, AutoSketch searches for an attach point near to the point selected. If one is found, that is used instead. Attach cannot work with grouped items, and may also affect the Point, Distance, Scale and Break commands.

Measure Menu
This menu is used to obtain dimensions and other measurements of parts of your drawings. It is also possible from this menu to add the dimensions to your drawing. The dimensions specified are calculated and displayed automatically, and once displayed, will be updated if any part of the drawing they refer to is changed.

Figure 1.5 is a screen-dump showing a simple example with some dimensions indicated.

Angle is used to indicate the angle between two bearings or directions. Three points are required, a base point and two directions. Typically, these would be the point at which two lines meet, and one point on each line. The indication will then be the angle between the two lines.

Area is used to calculate the area within a perimeter you specify. You specify the area by selecting a series of points. AutoSketch marks the first point with a large cross, and you finish indicating the area by selecting this point again. The measured area and the length of the perimeter is displayed. If any of the bounding sides of the area is curved, the area measurement can only be approximate, and the accuracy of this approximation depends to some extent on how many points on the curve you specify.

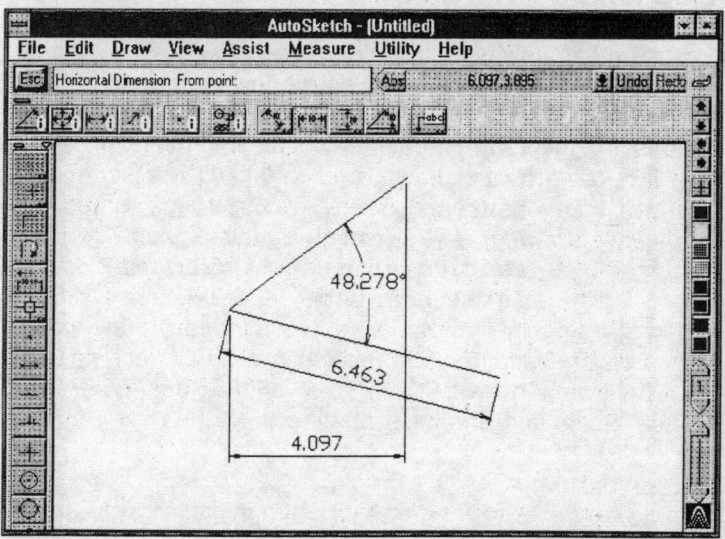

Figure 1.5. A drawing with dimensions included.

Distance simply calculates and displays the distance between two points on your drawing. This distance is stored in a 'system variable', /ldist, and this can be used when entering drawing commands from the keyboard. Use of system variables is covered in Chapter 2.

Bearing is similar to Angle, but it requires only two points, and it indicates the bearing or compass angle of the second from the first. Cartesian co-ordinates are used. The measured angle is stored in the /langle system variable.

Point causes the co-ordinates of a point to be displayed. Whenever you click the pointer with Point in force, a dialog box appears showing the co-ordinates of the pointer at the time you clicked. This can be used to find the exact position of any point in your drawing. The position is displayed in the current units.

Show Properties produces a dialog showing the current properties for any object in a drawing. The properties shown

15

will, of course, depend on the particular object selected. Figure 1.6 shows the dialog for a polyline.

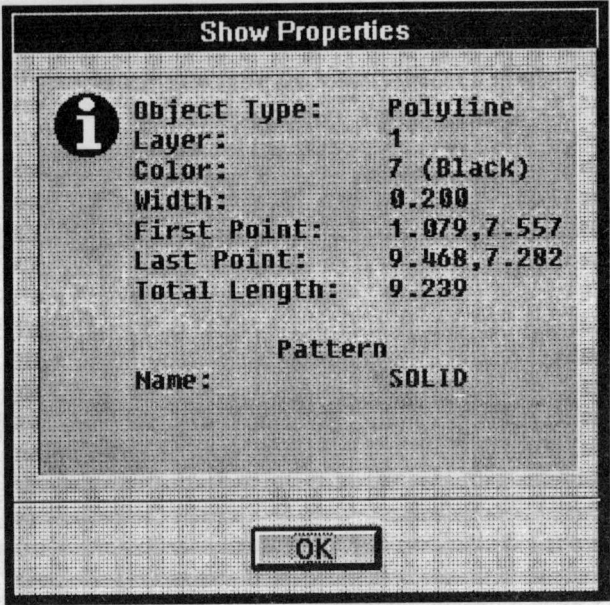

Figure 1.6. The Show Properties dialog.

Align Dimension, like the other commands in this menu suffixed with 'dimension', is used to actually insert a calculated dimension in your drawing. It is used to calculate and display the actual distance between two points.

Horiz. Dimension is used to calculate and display the horizontal distance between two points. The two points may also be vertically displaced. It is only the horizontal displacement which is indicated.

Vert. Dimension is used to calculate and display the vertical distance between two points. The two points may also be horizontally displaced. It is only the vertical displacement which is indicated.

Angle Dimension shows on the drawing the angle between two lines. The lines must not be parallel, but do not necessarily have to meet within the area of the drawing. You must select the two lines, and then indicate a point through which the dimensioning arc will be drawn. The arc will be broken to insert the text. If there is not enough room at the point you indicated, you will be prompted for another.

Utility Menu
The items on this menu are used to set up AutoSketch to your requirements, to set the properties for the drawing commands, and to perform various peripheral functions.

Drawing Settings lets you change the values and modes used by other commands, in particular some of those on the Assist menu, such as the grid size settings. It also lets you change settings for some drawing commands.

When you select this item, a dialogue box will appear, and you choose buttons in this dialog, according to what you want to change. Figure 1.7 shows this dialog.

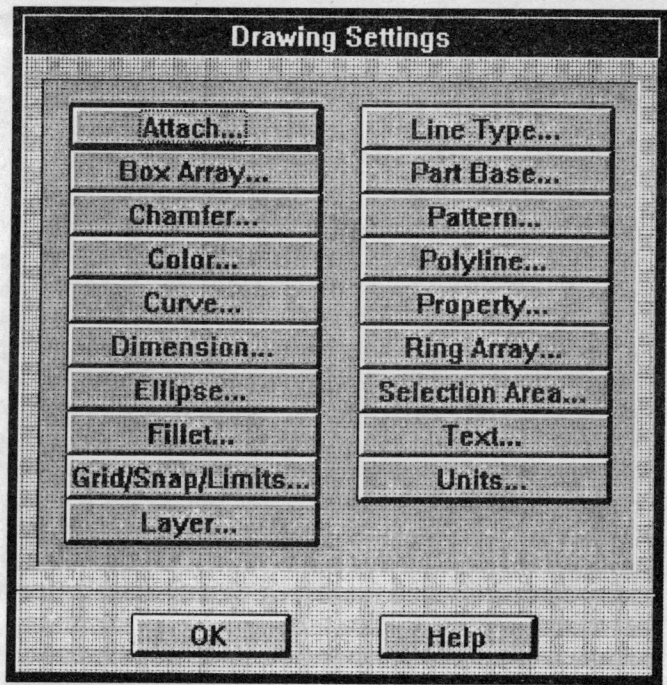

Figure 1.7. The Drawing Settings dialog.

Preferences produces a dialog box which allows you to set where AutoSketch will place the Undo file It also allows you to disable the Undo button, and disable selection highlighting. Figure 1.8 shows this dialog.

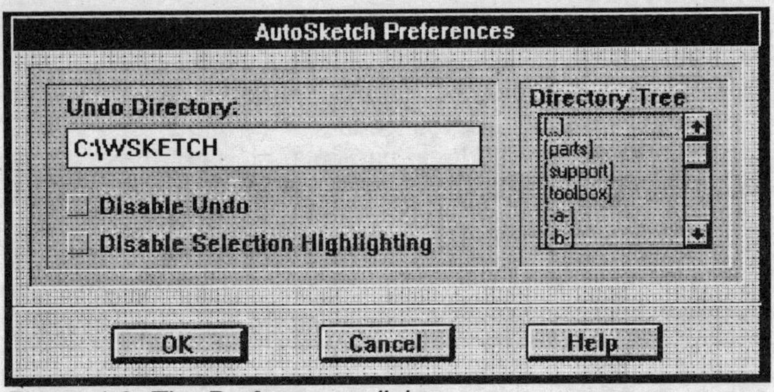

Figure 1.8. The Preferences dialog.

There are four commands on this menu which allow you to create and edit your own toolboxes. This allows you to group your own chosen sets of commands. There is also a button editor for these toolboxes. This is an advanced feature for users who like to personalise programs for their own requirements, and it falls outside the scope of this book.

Record Macro is used to send a series of AutoSketch commands to a file. This file can then be 'played' repeatedly. This can be used when you need to draw the same object several times, but it is not considered suitable for saving as a part file, or for sequences of commands you use frequently. For example, you can create a macro which you can use whenever starting a new drawing to set things like pen, grid and snap settings. You select this command from the menu, perform the actions you want to record (which can include making menu selections, drawing commands, and making dialog settings), and then select this command again to end the macro.

Play Macro causes AutoSketch to load and play back all the commands and actions stored in a macro file. When you choose this command, you will be presented with a dialog, from which you may select the macro to be played.

User Input is used only while recording a macro. Selecting this will cause the macro currently being recorded to pause when it is played back, and wait for user input. The user input can be either keyboard input, to pick a location or object, or to close a dialog box.

Copy BMP is used to copy part or all of a drawing to the Windows clipboard as a Windows bitmap. This can then be pasted into other Windows applications. The quality of this will, of course, be limited to screen resolution. In release 1 of AutoSketch for Windows, it is not possible to import bitmaps into AutoSketch drawings, or to save BMP files, but bitmap import is included in Release 2.

Copy WMF is used to copy part or all of the drawing to the clipboard in Windows Metafile format. The metafile rendering of the drawing may not be exactly the same as the AutoSketch printed version, but will be very close. AutoSketch for Windows Release 1 does not allow pasting or importing of metafiles, or saving files in WMF format, but metafile import is included in Release 2.

The last two items on this menu, Copy Object and Paste Object are concerned with Windows Object Linking and Embedding, and the use of these is beyond the scope of this book, except to say that many of the illustrations in this book are embedded objects within the word processor file.

The Help Menu
The help menu is a fairly standard Windows help menu, from where context-sensitive help can be obtained. Also on this menu is the SmartCursor toggle. SmartCursors indicate the function of buttons in toolboxes when the cursor is over them. This is likely to be a help when first using the program, until you come to recognise the icons.

The About AutoSketch option produces a dialog which will display the serial number and registration details of your copy. It also gives the release version and date.

The Example Drawings

AutoSketch comes with a number of example drawings. These give a good idea of the scope of the program, and are also useful for initial familiarisation. It is a good idea to load up these drawings and to explore them with the zoom and pan facilities. This will give you practice at moving around a large drawing. In particular, try the Zoom Box command. To use this, select the command, select a point to one corner of an interesting area, then move to the opposite corner of this area. As you do this, a box will be drawn. When you complete the command, the contents of this box will be zoomed to fill the whole screen. You may be surprised to find a great deal more detail than was apparent in the original view.

It is not unusual when using the Zoom commands initially to end up with an apparently empty screen. There are two causes of this, both of which stem from the fact that AutoSketch, like most CAD programs, can display drawings at a very wide range of magnifications.

If you use the Zoom Box command, and fumble slightly when selecting the area to zoom, you may accidentally draw a very small box. It is possible that this box may have nothing in it. Nonetheless, AutoSketch will quite successfully scale it to fill the screen, which of course will be empty.

A similar result can sometimes occur when using Zoom Limits. This fills the screen with the entire drawing area (i.e. the Drawing Limits as set from the Settings menu). It is possible to set very large drawing limits, and then, perhaps through confusion about units, use only a very small area of it. In this case, you will usually find, if you look closely, a small dot in the bottom left-hand corner (it can sometimes be elsewhere). This is your drawing, scaled down!

In either of these events, the usual recovery method is to choose either Last View or Zoom Full from the View menu. Last View is in effect an Undo command for zooms, and just takes you back to where you were. Zoom Full fills the screen with the area actually drawn on, whether this area is larger or smaller than the drawing limits. On the whole, Last View is safer.

It can also be useful to try printing the example drawings. This will give you some practice with print boxes, and sizing and scaling, and will also reveal any offset caused by the areas of paper in which your printer cannot print (all printers have such areas). It may be a good idea to read the last chapter in this book before trying this.

2. DRAWING

If you have ever used a computer 'paint' type program, you will probably have found that you can simply hold down the mouse button and start drawing freehand lines. If you try this with AutoSketch, you will find that all that happens is that the mouse pointer disappears as long as the button is down. Drawing techniques in CAD are quite different.

It is actually quite unusual for a true CAD program to have a provision for drawing freehand lines, though one or two do. In AutoSketch, all lines are drawn as straight lines or as curves or arc segments. Before you can draw anything, you must select a command from the Draw menu (or alternatively enter one from the keyboard). This is typical of the way CAD programs work.

The parts of a drawing which you create are termed objects. Each line, circle, arc, etc., is a separate object, even if they have been drawn to join up into complex figures. These objects can be individually selected for subsequent editing operations, such as those on the Change menu. It is possible to group objects so that they can be treated as if they were a single object for some purposes, such as moving and scaling, but the identities of the individual objects are not lost, and the items can be 'ungrouped' again.

This storage of 'objects' explains why very few CAD programs allow freehand drawing. A freehand line has to be stored as a series of small straight lines, each a separate object, and this can result in huge file sizes.

In AutoSketch, there are two ways of actually drawing. You can either use the mouse, graphics tablet or other pointing device, or you can type in drawing instructions and co-ordinates from the keyboard. The former is by far the most common method, but the latter should not be dismissed as useless, difficult, boring or impractical. There are circumstances when it is simply the easiest and best way of getting the job done.

That said, the use of a pointing device is the most common way of drawing, and that will be dealt with first.

Drawing with a Mouse

A mouse is the most frequently used pointing device on personal computers. It is perfectly usable for CAD, though perhaps not ideal. Most professional CAD users prefer a graphics tablet. However, a good graphics tablet is an expensive item, much more expensive than a mouse, and so may not appeal to beginners.

The most important thing if using a mouse is to ensure that the maximum precision is obtained. The more precision from the mouse, the smaller the scale you can work at, which means you will be able to see more of your drawing on the screen. This means using a good quality mouse mat, and ensuring that the mouse is kept clean. Dust picked up from the mouse mat can accumulate on the mouse ball and on the rollers inside the mouse, and this can lead to a jerky action, with some movement being lost, and the pointer then jumping a considerable distance with even the smallest mouse movement.

There are two common types of mouse mat. The most common has a flock surface on a foam rubber backing. With these, the surface tends to trap dust, so that it does not get carried up into the mouse. Mouse cleaning with these is an infrequent operation. The mat itself will benefit from an occasional wash.

The other type has a soft, smooth plastic surface, again with a foam backing. These can allow good control, but can be rather less satisfactory from the point of view of keeping the mouse clean. Both dust, and sweat and dead skin from the user's hand, will work up into the mouse, and more frequent cleaning may be necessary. If you have this type of mat, a sweep with a handkerchief before starting work can be a good idea. Fairly regular polishing of the mouse rollers with a dry cotton bud is generally adequate cleaning, and the mouse ball can be removed and rinsed under a warm tap, and dried with a grease and lint free cloth.

As an alternative to mechanical mice, there are optical mice, which need a special mat with an optical grid printed on it. These are more expensive than standard mice, and may need an external power supply, but cleaning problems do not arise, and they can be more accurate for CAD work.

24

Drawing Commands

The basic principle of drawing with the mouse is to select a command from the Draw menu, and then to select the point or points (depending on the command) at which you want to draw. The points are selected by moving the mouse pointer to the appropriate place and clicking.

For example, to draw a straight line, you select the Line command, move the mouse pointer to one end point, click, move the mouse pointer to the other end, and click again. You do not need to hold the mouse button down while moving between the two points, as you usually do with 'paint' programs.

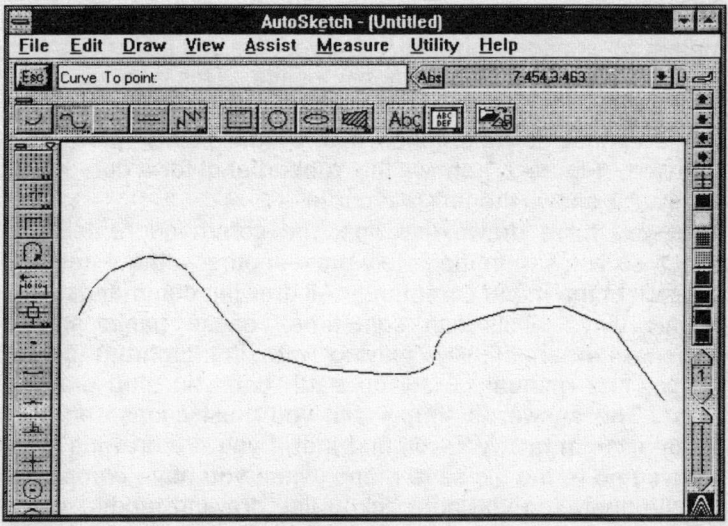

Figure 2.1. A curve 'rubberband'.

Note that when drawing a series of lines in succession, each line requires a start point and an end point. The command does not work in a point-to-point-to-point fashion like the line drawing in many paint programs. However, if you want to do this, it is one of the facilities of the polyline command. Otherwise, you can use a double click to end each line and begin the next at the same point, if you need a series of connected normal lines. This may feel strange at first for paint program users, as with these a double click is often used to end a sequence of lines. Note that this will not reliably give precise alignment, as it is possible to move the mouse slightly between clicks. Methods of ensuring accurate alignment are given below.

After you have selected the first point, as you move the mouse a temporary guide line, called a 'rubberband' line, is drawn from that point to the current position of the mouse cursor. This is a guide, to show you what will be drawn.

All drawing commands have some form of rubberbanding, but the accuracy of the representation varies somewhat from command to command. With circles, for example, the rubberband takes a polygonal shape, rather than being a true circle (the latest Windows versions do show a circle). This is mainly to speed things up. Curves are initially shown as straight lines between the chosen points. This is again partly for speed, but also because, with spline curves, the final shape cannot be determined until all the points have been selected. Figure 2.1 shows the 'rubberband' for a curve, and Figure 2.2 shows the finished curve.

After you have drawn one line, the command remains in effect, so you can immediately draw another without needing to reselect the menu command. All drawing commands work in this way. This can sometimes cause panic among beginners when initially 'playing' with the program before reading the manual. How on earth can you stop drawing lines! The answer is simply that you must choose another command. In fact, you will find that if you are drawing lines and you go to the file save menu, when you have completed the file operation you are back in line drawing mode. Once you have started drawing, there is no way of explicitly turning all drawing commands off. The prompt line will always indicate the command in force, and what action you are expected to take next.

With commands which can take a variable number of points, like curves and polylines, some way is needed of telling the program when you have finished the object. The normal way of doing this is to select the same point twice. If this fails to work, it could be that you have moved the mouse very slightly between the two clicks. (The Attach mode described later largely overcomes this problem.)

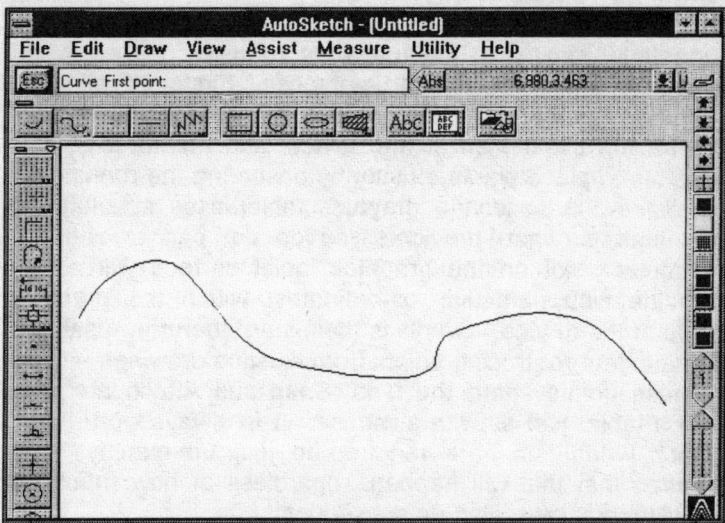

Figure 2.2. The finished curve.

CAD differs from artistic computer graphics in the degree of precision which is required. Where working drawings are being produced, dimensions must be exact. If such drawings are to be produced with a mouse, the mouse must be capable of giving this degree of precision. It is in the nature of a mouse, however, that it is not capable of this. You can demonstrate this by using the mouse with running co-ordinates turned on. You will find it very hard to adjust the figures to exact values by moving the mouse.

The mouse is essentially a screen-pointing device. It is solely designed to move a pointer on the screen, and the co-ordinates the mouse driver produces are scaled to this end. In CAD, a higher resolution than this is often required. CAD drawings can be scaled up and down between wide limits, and to allow for scaling up, points in drawings must be placed with more precision than can be shown on the screen. There are several aids provided in AutoSketch to help with this.

Graphics Tablets

The techniques of drawing using a graphics tablet are essentially similar to the use of a mouse. However, the graphics tablet has two advantages. Firstly, it allows a greater degree of precision in controlling the pointer. This is inherent in the design of the device, and means it is often possible to place points exactly by observing the running co-ordinates. Secondly, a graphics tablet uses absolute co-ordinates, so that, provided you do not pan or zoom, a particular point on the graphics tablet surface will always coincide with particular co-ordinates, within the precision limits of the device. Graphics tablets are therefore usable to some extent for tracing points from existing drawings.

These points apart, the Grid, Snap and Attach are used with a tablet just as with a mouse. It is always worth using Attach when lines are required to join up exactly, as it ensures that this will happen, regardless of how much the drawing may be scaled up subsequently.

Grid and Snap

Grid and Snap are the two most useful drawing aids when using a mouse. In fact, you will probably find you use them most of the time. Though in AutoSketch they are used and set independently, they are normally used together. Both Grid and Snap are off by default, so if you create a startup macro to set your preferences, you may find it convenient to include grid and snap settings in it.

Grid places a regularly-spaced matrix of dots on the screen. These dots can then be used for lining up parts of the drawing, and also to size items. The grid size is set in drawing units, and will scale up and down with the drawing. Care is needed here. If you scale up too far, the whole screen area can be less than the space between dots, so that none are visible. In the other direction, the grid will be turned off automatically if the dot-spacing becomes too small for reasonable display on the screen. The dots do not reappear automatically when you return to a larger scale, and you must turn the grid back on yourself.

Snap can be set and used independently of the grid, but it is much more normal to use them together. When Snap is on, you effectively have two pointers on the screen. One is the normal mouse pointer, the other is a small cross-hair cursor. The mouse pointer moves normally, but the cursor is constrained to move only to fixed points as specified by the snap setting. As you move the mouse pointer, the cursor follows it, jumping to the nearest snap point. If running co-ordinates are on, they indicate the position of the cursor.

When you select a point by clicking the mouse, it is the position of the cursor, not the pointer, which is used for drawing. In this way, while Snap is on, all drawing points are aligned with the snap points, so high drawing precision can be obtained quickly and easily. Of course, if you need to draw to points not on the snap matrix, you need either to temporarily turn Snap off, or to adjust the settings to smaller intervals. Doing either of these will have no effect on what you have already drawn.

To anyone used to computer painting programs, which also normally have a snap feature, the flexibility of CAD programs can come as a surprise. On painting programs, grid and snap usually go together, and you can't have one without the other. The grid settings are the same as the snap settings. Also, the spacing of the grid in the x and y directions must often be the same. In AutoSketch, Grid and Snap are set independently, can use quite separate matrix dimensions, and can both have different settings in the two directions.

Whether all this flexibility is frequently used is another matter. It is probably true to say that most users, most of the time, use Grid and Snap together, with the same settings, and with equal intervals in x and y directions! However, differential settings do have their uses. Normally, it is more useful to have snap set finer than the grid. For example, if you have the snap and grid setting the same, and you draw a square four units by four units, and you need to draw to the centre of this square, there is no problem. On the other hand, if the square must be five by five, then you do have a problem! It will, in fact, frequently be found useful to have the snap spacing half that of the grid spacing. Figure 2.3 shows a drawing where this has been done to align a line and the centre of a circle with the centre point of a five-unit square.

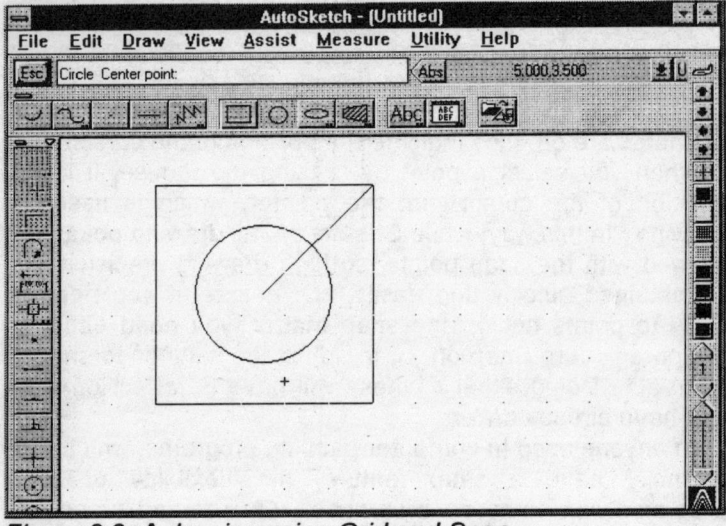

Figure 2.3. A drawing using Grid and Snap.

Snap and Grid are both set from the Settings menu. Selecting either of these produces a dialog box, shown in Figure 2.4. The method of setting is identical for the two features. There are three settings to be made, the two spacings and the on/off toggle. The x-spacing should always be set first. It is automatically copied to the y-spacing, so if you want the two to be the same, as is usual, only the one figure needs to be entered. If you want different settings and you set the y setting first, it will be changed when you enter the x figure. Making these settings does not of itself cause the grid to appear or snap to come into effect. You must turn the feature on by clicking the box, and then click on OK to clear the dialog box. If you click on Cancel, the new settings will be discarded and the previous settings will remain in effect. During drawing, you can use the On/Off setting in the dialog box to temporarily turn grid or snap on or off, without losing the spacing settings. You can toggle snap on and off with Alt + F7, and grid with Alt + F6. Both grid and snap can also be turned on and off from the Assist menu.

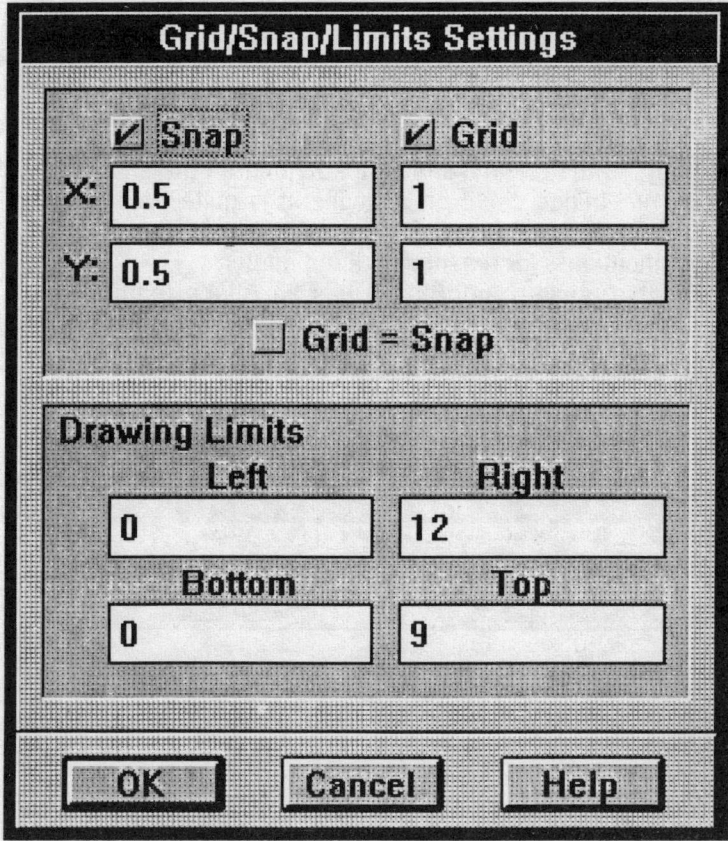

Figure 2.4. The Grid/Snap Dialog.

If you want the grid and snap settings to be the same, you can simply set the grid settings to zero. When you turn the grid on, the snap spacing will then be used. If you alter the snap setting subsequently, this will be reflected in the grid spacing automatically.

Of course, the grid is only an aid to drawing. It is never printed or plotted, and it never appears as part of a slide if you save your drawing in this form. If you need to show the grid for any reason, the only way is by means of a screen dump.

Attach

There will frequently be times when you want one line to join on exactly to another line. If the original line has been drawn using snap (and you have not changed the snap setting) this is easy. If the original line is not aligned on the snap matrix, however, things could be difficult. It is quite hard to move the pointer to the exact end of a line, even at high magnifications, for reasons outlined earlier.

For this reason, AutoSketch has an Attach feature, which helps in this and similar circumstances. Where snap makes the cursor jump to predefined positions on a matrix, attach makes the pointer move to a position on an item already drawn. It can be used to find the ends of lines, and also seven other types of 'attach point'.

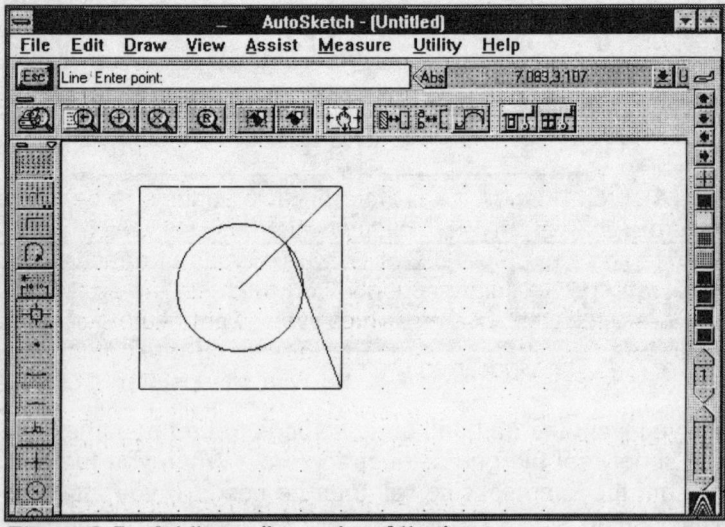

Figure 2.5. Adding a line using Attach.

Figure 2.5 shows how Attach can be used for accurate alignment. It is Figure 2.3 with a line added from where the original line from the centre point crosses the circle, to the corner of the box. Figure 2.6 is this drawing zoomed in so that the accuracy of alignment can be seen. You will see that the precision is exact, despite the fact that the line was added at the zoom factor of Figure 2.5

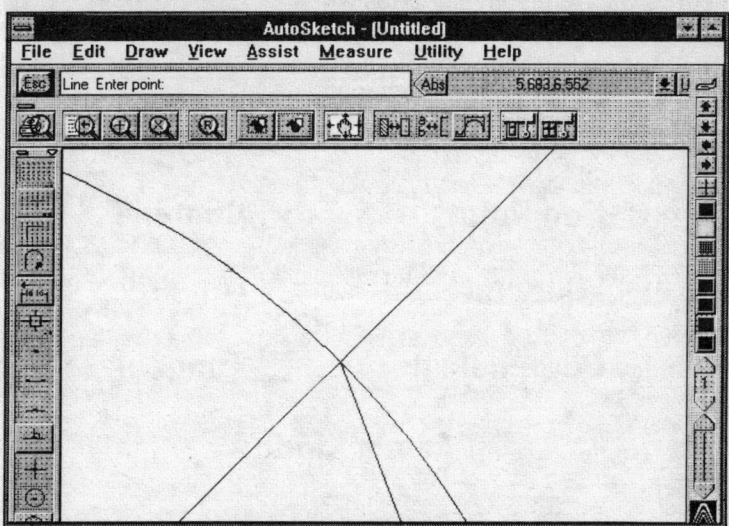

Figure 2.6. A zoomed view of Figure 2.5.

Apart from turning it on, there are two settings to be made in order to use attach. Firstly, you must set which attach modes you want to use (that is, which types of attach points you want to find), and secondly, you must set the size of the area around the pointer which you want AutoSketch to search for an attach point. The larger you make this area, the less precise you need to be with the pointer. On the other hand, a large *pick interval,* as it is called, may cause problems with several possible attach points occurring in the area.

You can turn the attach modes on and off individually, so you can use them singly or in any combination. Having more than one mode set increases the likelihood of more

33

than one possible attach point occurring in the pick interval. It is usually most efficient either to have a large pick interval and only one or two modes set, or a small pick interval and several modes set, but which to use depends on the nature of the drawing and the type of work you are doing. Only experience can provide the answer here.

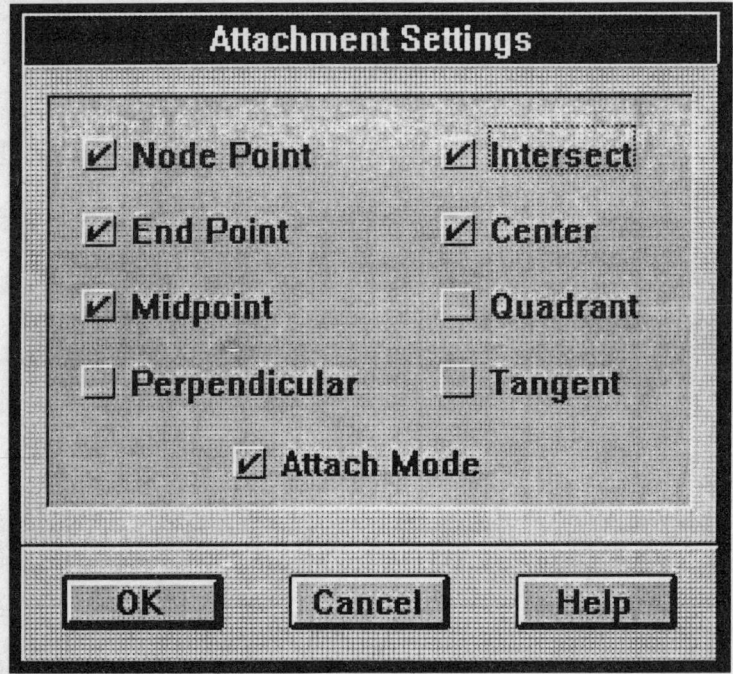

Attachment Settings

☑ **Node Point**   ☑ **Intersect**

☑ **End Point**   ☑ **Center**

☑ **Midpoint**   ☐ **Quadrant**

☐ **Perpendicular**   ☐ **Tangent**

☑ **Attach Mode**

[**OK**]   [**Cancel**]   [**Help**]

Figure 2.7. The Attach dialog.

Attach Modes
The attach modes are set in a dialog box which is produced by selecting Attach from the Assist menu. Attach mode can also be turned on and off in this dialog. Any combination of modes can be set. As usual, you must click on OK to close the dialog and bring the changes into effect. Clicking on cancel causes the settings to be discarded and the previous

settings remain in effect. Figure 2.7 shows the Attach dialog.

The eight modes are as follows.

Center finds the centre of circles and arcs, and also the centres of ellipses.

End Point finds the ends of lines, polyline segments, box line segments, curve frames if they are displayed, dimensions, pattern fill segments and arcs. This is probably the most frequently used mode.

Intersect needs two objects to work. It finds the point or points where the two objects cross.

Midpoint will find the middle of lines, polyline segments, curve frames, pattern fill segments and arcs. It is inappropriate for objects such as ellipses, text and circles which have no midpoint as such.

Node Point will find points, and the end points of text object baselines. It is sometimes useful to draw points (with the Point command on the Draw menu) purely to allow other objects to be attached to them with this mode. You can, for example, set a point from which a series of lines will radiate.

Perpendicular is one of the two attach modes which require two points. It is used with arcs, circles and ellipses, boxes, lines, polylines, pattern fill boundaries, and curve frames. The first point selects the object. When the second point is selected, AutoSketch finds a point on the original object such that a line drawn from the second point would be perpendicular to the object at the point of contact.

Quadrant finds the quadrant points on arcs and circles. It can also be used with ellipses, where it finds the ends of the semi-major and semi-minor axes.

Tangent is another attach mode which requires two points. As with Perpendicular, the first point selects an object, which must be a circle, ellipse or arc. When the second point is selected, AutoSketch finds a point on the original object such that a line drawn from the second point would be a tangent to the object.

The pick interval is set from the Pick command in the Settings menu. The interval is set not in drawing units, but rather as a percentage of the screen height. This avoids problems when zooming to larger or smaller scales. The default setting is 1%, which, on a 640x480 pixel VGA screen means an area of roughly 6 pixels by 5. This is in general a pretty good default. Setting a smaller figure will make it possible to select out points which are close together, but this needs care. A larger area makes less precision necessary when points are not closely spaced, but doesn't make things that much easier. Often, it is better to change the scale at which you are viewing the drawing rather than changing the pick interval.

Though the pick interval is normally described as the area which is searched for an attach point, in some cases it is more true to say it is the area searched for an object on which an attach point may be found. For example, if you have endpoint and midpoint modes turned on, and you move the pointer to anywhere on a line, with nothing else within the pick interval, the pointer will snap to either one of the ends or to the middle of the line, whichever is nearer to the original position of the pointer. However, if there is another possible attach point within the pick interval, this will be chosen rather than any point on the line.

Though attach modes can be used in any combination, they do have different priorities. If you have difficulty attaching to the type of point you require, try turning off all modes except the one you are trying to use. It is also a good idea to select a point as close as possible to where you think the attach point is. This is especially important with the perpendicular and tangent modes, which have the lowest priority, and which are the most 'difficult' for the program.

Zoom
Zoom is used to change the size at which you are drawing. There are several choices on the View menu, but the most useful for a quick increase in size for detailed drawing is Zoom Box. To use this, you draw a box around the part of the drawing you wish to work on by moving the pointer to one corner, clicking, and moving to the diagonally opposite corner of the area. You may move the pointer in any direction. Clicking again ends the operation, and the screen will be redrawn to show the new area. The F10 key can be used to select this command quickly.

The area you select does not need to match the screen shape. The program will ensure everything you include in the box is shown on the screen after zooming.

You can move back to the previous view quickly by using Last View on the View menu. The F9 key is the quick shortcut for this.

Zoom is not a reliable way of precisely aligning points. It is really so you can work at a convenient scale for the part of the job in hand. It is adequate if you are working on a drawing which will not be scaled up greatly and where exact alignment is not required.

When precise alignment is essential, the only ways are by using Snap or Attach, or by entering exact co-ordinates from the keyboard (see below).

Drawing with Keyboard Commands

As an alternative to using a pointing device, drawing co-ordinates can be entered directly from the keyboard. This is different to using the cursor keys as a pointing device. It involves typing in the exact co-ordinates of the points in your drawing.

This sounds difficult and boring, and wholly impractical, but there are times when it works rather well, and when it can be the preferred method, even if you have a pointing device. The best example of this is when you need to produce a drawing of a 'thing', and you have the object and a ruler in your hand. As you measure the object, it is much easier to type the dimensions in directly as drawing commands than to do the drawing with the mouse or whatever.

Drawing commands cannot be typed in from the keyboard. That is, you cannot type in 'Line' to draw a line. You must still choose Line from the Draw menu, either using the pointer or using the keyboard shortcut. All the actual drawing commands (except for the text commands) do have keyboard shortcuts. When drawing from the keyboard, the overlay for the function keys provided with AutoSketch can prove invaluable.

Once you have selected a drawing command, you will be prompted for the co-ordinates. For example, after selecting the line command, you will see

Line   From point:

on the command line. You then type in the x and y co-ordinate values, using a comma as a separator. For example, to start your line three units from the left and four units up, you would enter

 3,4

The command line will then show

Line   To point:

indicating that it now requires the co-ordinates of the other end. To draw the line to a point five units from the left and two up, you would enter

 5,2

As an alternative, relative co-ordinates can be used. In other words, you can enter the distance of the new point from the last point entered. This is done by enclosing the figures in parentheses (which most people call brackets), preceded by an 'R'. For example, the equivalent to the last example above using relative co-ordinates would be

 R(2,-2)

Note that relative co-ordinates can be negative as well as positive.

AutoSketch records certain data in so-called *system variables*. Four of these are of particular use when entering drawing commands. They all have names beginning with a backslash and the letter 'l'.

/langle stores the last angle measured using the Angle or Bearing features in the Measure menu.

/lpoint stores the last co-ordinates entered.

/lx and **/ly** store the x and y components of the last point you entered.

If, for example, you are drawing a series of connected lines, you need to enter two sets of co-ordinates for the first line only. For subsequent lines, you can enter /lpoint for the first point, and this ensures that the lines will connect correctly.

Note that all the items on the Assist menu are only applicable to drawing with a pointing device. When you draw by entering co-ordinates, lines will always be drawn exactly as entered, within the limits of accuracy of AutoSketch.

Figure 2.8 is a drawing of an old-style 5.25 inch disk. This was drawn (in actual size) entirely by typing in the co-ordinates, in quite a short time.

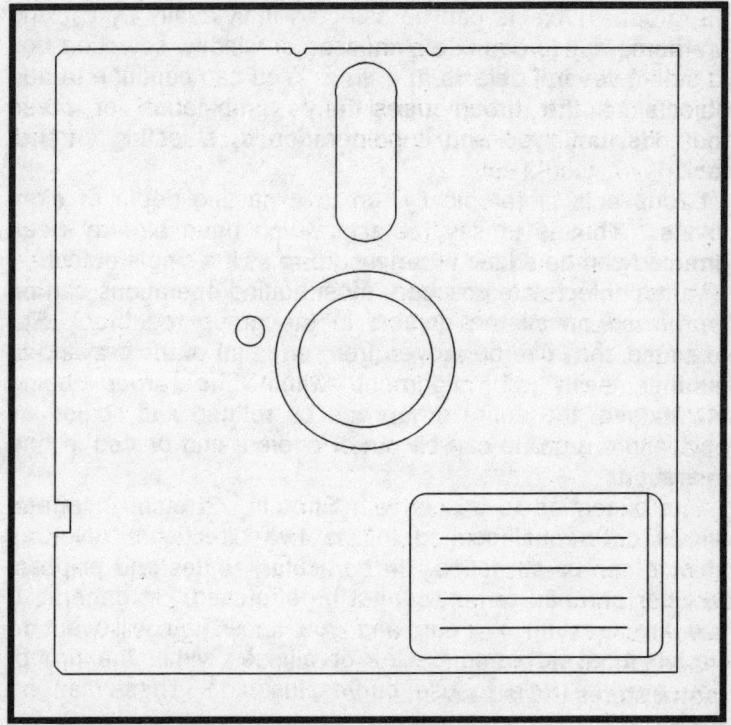

Figure 2.8. A keyboard-command drawing.

Group and Ungroup
Every item you draw in a drawing is stored as a separate item, and can be changed or deleted as a separate item. However, sometimes it is desirable to treat several of these component parts as if they were a single entity. If there are many aligned points, for example, and it is desired to move part of a drawing to another place, it would be difficult and

time consuming to do this a line at a time, and then re-align all the points.

Group (on the Edit menu) allows you to do this. You select Group from the menu, or by using the keys Alt+F9 on the keyboard, and then select the objects you wish to include in the group. Objects can be selected individually by clicking on them, or you can use a crosses or window selection box to select several objects at a time. You can continue to add objects to the group using any combination of these methods, until you end the operation by selecting another tool.

Group acts hierarchically, up to a nesting depth of eight levels. That is to say, objects which have already been grouped can be added to a new group as if a single object.

When objects are grouped, most editing operations can be performed on all the objects in the group together. For example, they can be moved from one part of the drawing to another, with all alignment within the group being maintained, the entire group can be rotated and scaled as one, and the group can be cut or copied, and pasted in one operation.

The exception to this is with Stretch. Stretch, in effect, allows differential scaling in the two directions. Not all objects can be stretched. In particular, circles and ellipses, whether grouped or not, cannot be stretched. In general, if you are creating a group and you know you will want to stretch it, avoid using circles or ellipses within the group. You may be able to use curves instead. These can be stretched.

If you do stretch a group containing a circle or ellipse, the aspect ratio of this object will not alter, but the position of the object relative to other objects, may change, depending on how the stretch is performed. Stretch treats each object in a group as a separate object, so results may not be as desired. If you use Stretch with groups, expect to use Undo fairly frequently.

Ungroup is the opposite to Group. It allows the objects within a group to be treated as separate objects again. This is useful to allow selective removal of objects from groups, among other things. To use Ungroup, you select the command from the Edit menu (the keyboard shortcut is Alt+F10), and then select the group in any of the usual ways. The objects will then be treated as individual objects.

Note, however, that Ungroup also works hierarchically. If you grouped a number of objects, then drew, say, five more objects, and then used Group again, selecting the original group and these five objects, the first use of Ungroup would separate out the five new objects but leave the original group intact. A second use of Ungroup will be necessary to allow the objects in the original to be edited individually. Using hierarchical grouping in this way can be a very useful tool.

Mirror

Mirror allows part of a drawing to be duplicated, but reversed about a mirroring line, like seeing an original and a reflection in a mirror. This can be useful to obtain symmetry. Normally, with the drawing aids available, symmetry is easy, but it can be hard work with curves, and Mirror may make it easier.

When you use mirror, you specify a *mirror line*. This line is not drawn, but the copy of your selected objects is drawn on the opposite side of this line to the original, with all points equidistant. The mirror line does not need to be exactly vertical or horizontal. If it is not, AutoSketch will rotate the copy to the required angle.

Mirror will reverse everything in the copy except text and fill patterns. Text will read normally. Neither the letters nor the order of letters will be changed. However, in blocks of formatted text, justification will be reversed. Left justification becomes right justification and *vice versa*. Most fill patterns are symmetrical, but with those that are not, no reversal occurs and this may spoil the mirror effect.

Figures 2.9, 2.10 and 2.11 show the effects of horizontal, vertical and angled mirroring.

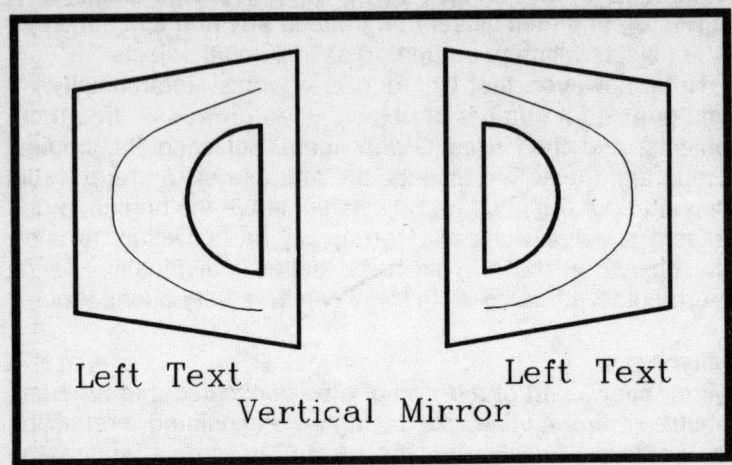

Figure 2.9. Vertical mirroring.

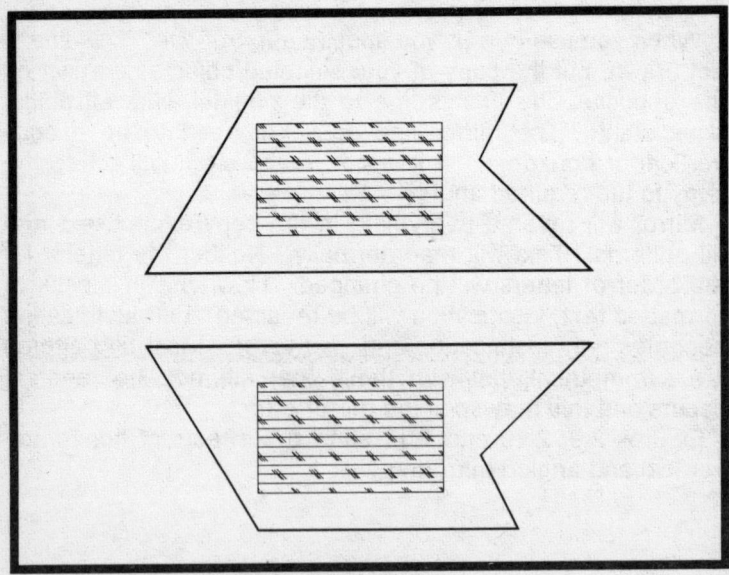

Figure 2.10. Horizontal mirroring.

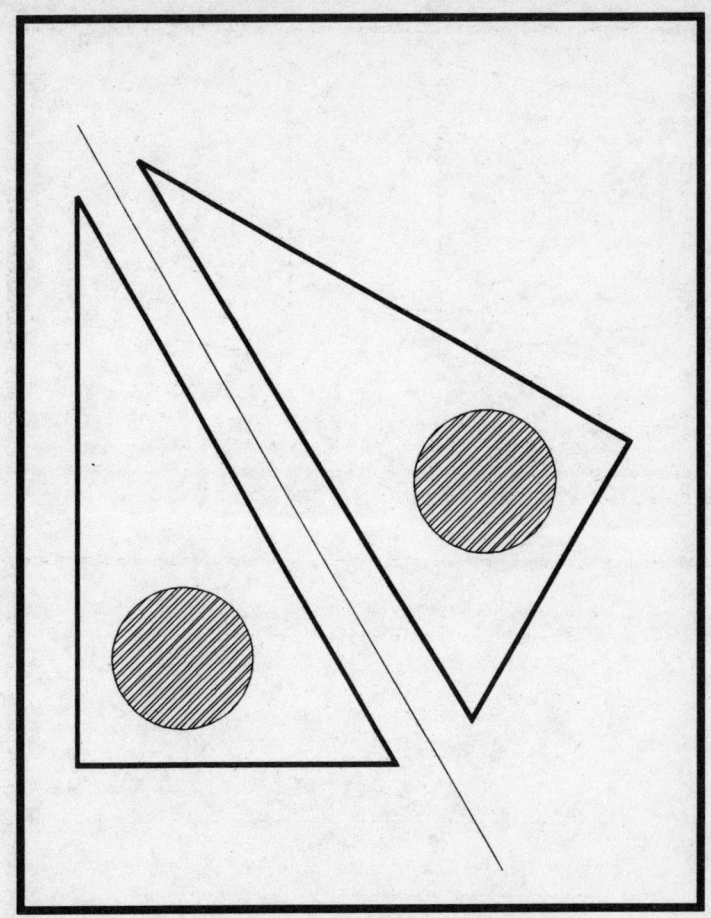

Figure 2.11. Angled mirroring (mirror line shown).

3. OBJECTS

In this chapter we will look a the objects which go to make up drawings. We will see how to draw them and how to use them in drawings, and how they fit together. We will also learn about the properties of objects. This chapter therefore deals mostly with the items on the Draw menu.

Line

The line is the simplest of objects in a drawing. It is simply a straight line between two points. If a series of connected lines is required, each component line is a separate object. Lines do not have a width. They are regarded as having zero width, but are rendered on the printer as a line one pixel (printer dot) wide. On a plotter, the width will be that of the pen used. Having lines as fine as possible is of advantage in technical drawings from which measurements may be made.

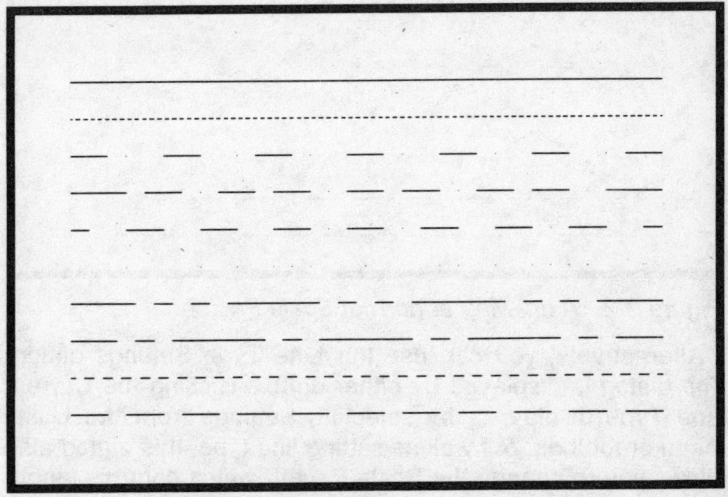

Figure 3.1. Available line types.

Lines can be drawn in a number of line types. These include most of the types used in conventional technical drawing, including dashed, dotted, and combinations of these, as well as, of course, solid. You must select the line type to be used before drawing the line(s), though it can be altered subsequently by using Change on the Edit menu.

The line type can be selected quickly by using the Current Line Type display to the bottom left of the screen border. This displays a short vertical sample of the current line type, with an arrowhead button at each end. You can cycle quickly through the available types by clicking on these buttons. Figure 3.1 shows all the available line types.

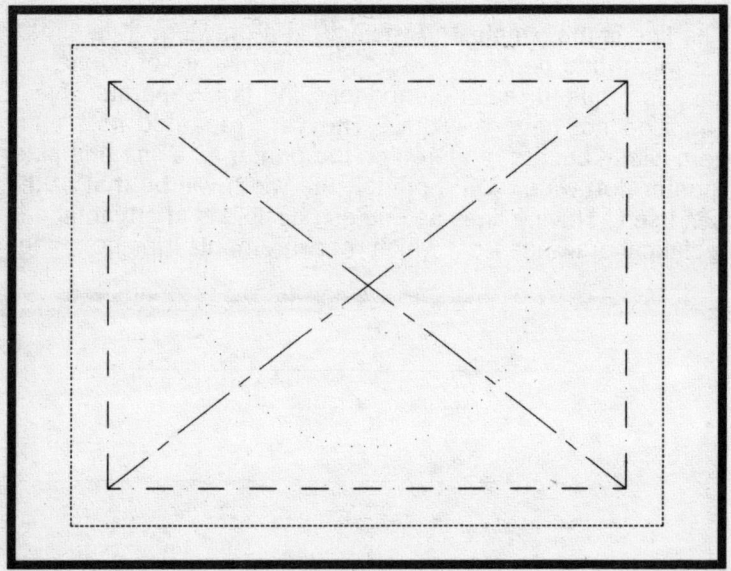

Figure 3.2. A drawing at normal Scale Factor.

Alternatively, you can use the Line Type Settings dialog. The dialog is displayed by either double-clicking the Current Line Type display, or by selecting Settings from the Utility menu or toolbox. As well as setting line type, this dialog also allows you to change the Scale Factor, which controls length of dashes and dot spacings. If all line types appear as solid on your drawing, you need to increase the scale factor. If they appear too 'open', you need to reduce it.

There is only one scale factor for the whole drawing. If you alter it, all existing lines will be redrawn to reflect the change. You are only likely to need to do this if you change the drawing limits. Figures 3.2 and 3.3 show the effect of a scale factor change.

Polylines
Polylines are lines which can have considerably more properties than ordinary lines. Firstly, they can be in sections. A series of connected lines can be drawn as a single polyline object. Secondly, polylines can have a definite width. This is useful for drawings which are to be photocopied, where bold lines may be desirable. Thirdly, polylines do not need to be solid black. They can have a pattern fill. This is very useful with really wide polylines. Figure 3.4 shows some straight polylines of varying widths.

As well as straight line segments, it is possible to include arc segments within a polyline. The arcs do not need to be separate objects. They can be included as segments in a polyline which also contains straight lines and/or other arcs. AutoSketch does not have a facility for a wide-line circle, but this can be produced using polyline by drawing it as two

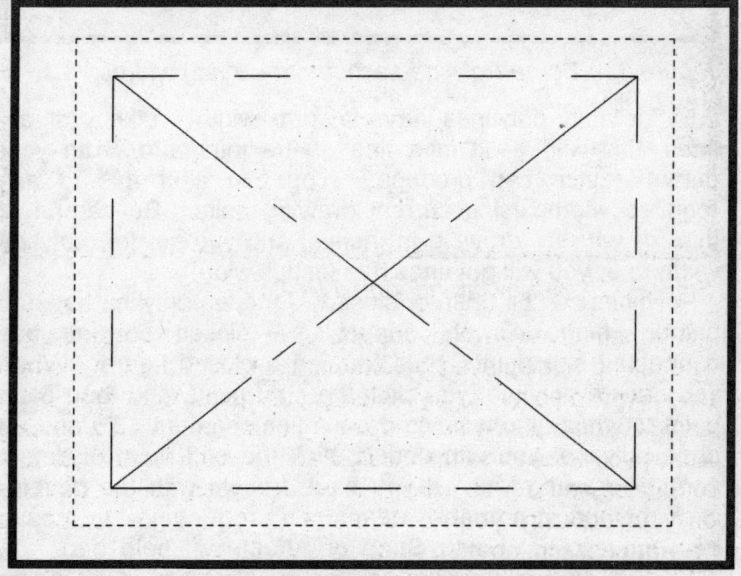

Figure 3.3. The same drawing at a higher Scale Factor.

47

semicircular arcs or similar.

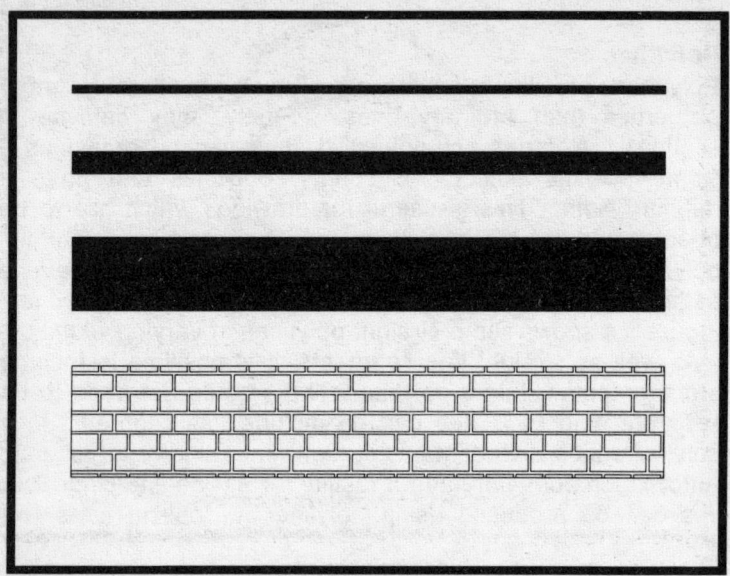

Figure 3.4. Some Polyline sections of varying widths.

By default, polylines have a zero width. Like ordinary lines, this will result in a line of the minimum width your output device can produce. You can alter this to any required width, using current drawing units. Be careful of this. If you are drawing in inches, and you set the polyline width to 5, you will get lines five inches wide!

Polylines can be open or closed. An open polyline has end points which do not connect. A closed polyline has connected end points, thus forming a closed figure. When you draw a polyline, you click the start point, and then each point to which you want to draw a line segment. To end an open polyline, you can double-click the end point or select another drawing tool. If you have trouble with the double-click method, it probably means you are moving the mouse between clicks. Using Snap or Attach will help here. A closed polyline will be ended automatically when you click on the start point again. Snap or Attach will again make it easier to obtain the necessary precision.

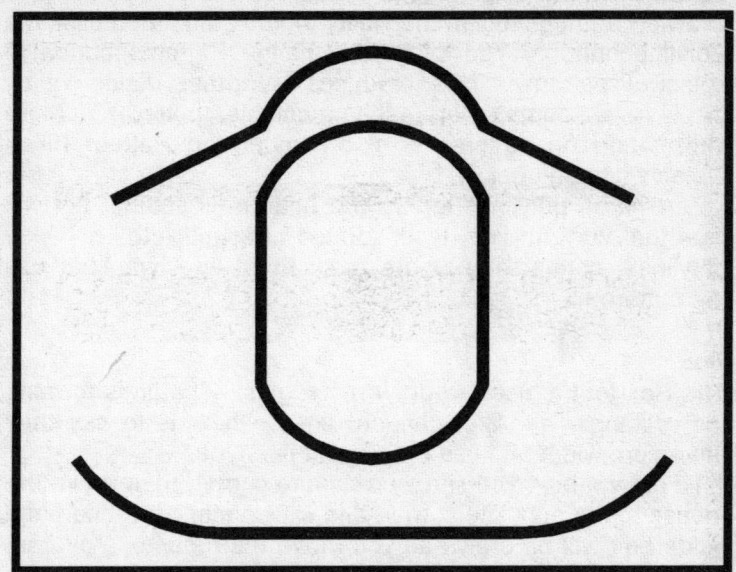

Figure 3.5. Open and closed Polylines.

An arc segment can be drawn at any time within a polyline. To switch to drawing arcs, you can select Arc Mode from the Assist menu or toolbox, or you can use the keyboard shortcut Ctrl + F1. Figure 3.5 shows open and closed polylines including arc sections.

The start point of the arc will be the last point drawn in the polyline. (If you want to start a polyline with an arc, set the start point before selecting arc mode.) You must then click a point on the arc to set the radius, and then the end point of the arc. To switch back to line segments again, you can either select Arc Mode again (it acts as an on-off toggle) or press Ctrl + F1 again.

Wide polylines can have a pattern fill rather than a solid fill. To do this successfully, the lines need to be wide enough to show the pattern properly. If the lines are too narrow, the effect will appear rather random, and will tend to look as if something has gone wrong with the printer.

The width and fill pattern for polylines are set from the Polyline Settings dialog. To display this you can either double-click the Polyline tool in the Draw toolbox, or click the Drawing Settings tool in the Utility toolbox, and then click the Polyline button. You click the Change Patterns button to select a pattern. This produces a further dialog which displays a sample of each available pattern. More information on patterns is given under the Pattern Filled Objects heading below.

Zero-width polylines ignore the pattern-fill setting, but will use the current line type (dotted, dashed etc.). Wide polylines, conversely, ignore the current line type, but use the pattern fill.

Box

The Box tool is used to draw rectangles. The lines forming the rectangle are like standard lines, which is to say they have zero width and use the current line type.

To draw a box, you simply click one corner, then move the mouse to the opposite corner, and click again. A rubberband guide box will be drawn as you move the mouse. You can, of course, also enter the co-ordinates of the corners from the keyboard. You can make any of the four corners the first point, and move the mouse in any direction. You do not have to go from top-left to bottom-right, though most people will probably find this the most natural way. Co-ordinates can also be entered from the keyboard.

Boxes can only be drawn as rectangular 'ortho' boxes, with vertical and horizontal sides. However, once drawn, it is possible to rotate them using Rotate on the Edit menu or toolbox, or to distort them into non-rectangular shapes using Stretch.

Figure 3.6 includes boxes, including one which has been stretched to a non-rectangular shape.

Circle

The Circle tool draws circles using standard zero-width lines. The current line type (dotted, dashed, solid, etc.) is used.

To draw the circle, you first set the centre point by clicking with the mouse, and then move the mouse to a point on the circle and click again. The co-ordinates of the points can also be entered from the keyboard.

A rubberband guide circle is drawn as the mouse is moved. This guide is not drawn as accurately as the finished circle, and on early versions of AutoSketch, it was distinctly polygonal. Therefore, if you want the circle to pass through a particular point, click the mouse on that point. Do not rely on the fact that the rubberband circle passes through it, as the final circle may be slightly different.

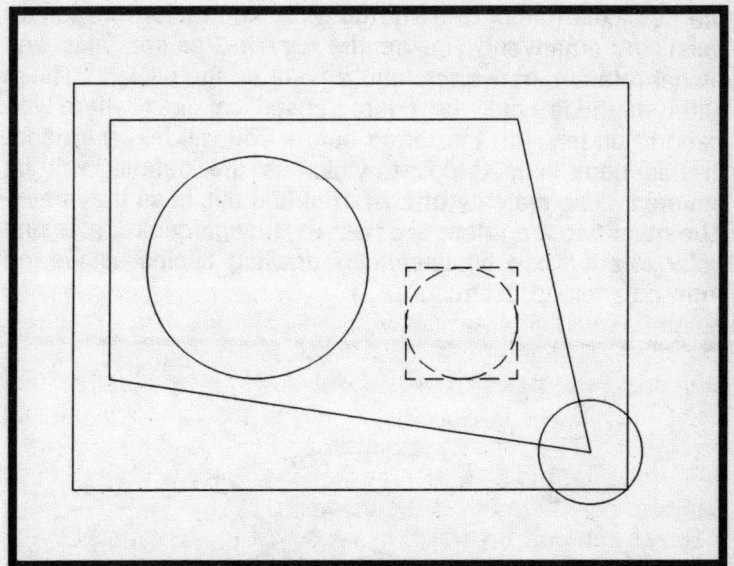

Figure 3.6. Boxes and Circles.

You cannot use Stretch to distort a circle. Circles will always remain circular. If you use Stretch and include the whole of the circle in the crosses/window selection box, it will be moved. If you enclose only part of the circle, it will be unaffected (this also applies to circles included in groups).

Figure 3.6 shows some circles, with both solid and dotted outlines.

Ellipse

The Ellipse tool is used to draw ellipses. Like boxes and circles, these are drawn using zero-width lines and the current line type.

Three ways of drawing ellipses are provided. Probably the most commonly used way is to specify the centre point and the two axes (minor, the shorter axis, and major, the longer axis). Alternatively, you can specify the centre, axis and planar rotation, or two foci and a point on the ellipse. These latter methods could be characterised as ones where you need to understand the terms before you will feel the need! In this book only the first, which is the default, will be covered. The majority of users will find this is all they need. The other two are rather specialised, though centre, axis and polar rotation can be useful for drawing circles as viewed from an angle (3-D effects).

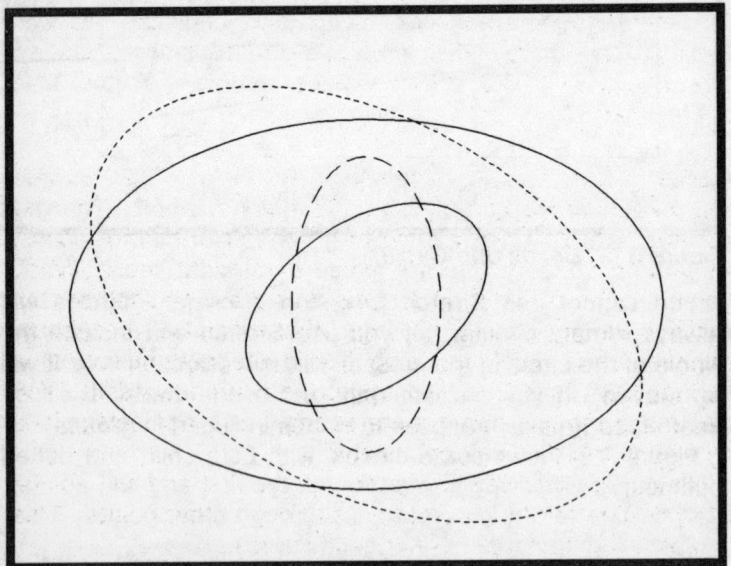

Figure 3.7. Ellipses.

To draw an ellipse by the default method, you first click on the centre of the ellipse. You then move the mouse to the required end point of one of the axes (it does not matter which) and click. You then move the mouse away from this point. As you do so, a rubberband guide ellipse is drawn. This is rather more rough than the circle rubberband guide. The other axis length is set as the perpendicular distance from the first axis to the current mouse position. You click the mouse when this is correct. It follows that the point at which you click does not need to be at the exact end of the axis, and it also does not, therefore, need to be on the ellipse. The co-ordinates can also be entered from the keyboard.

The axes do not need to be aligned horizontal and vertical. The point at which you set the end of the first axis sets the orientation of the ellipse. If you want to ensure horizontal and vertical axes, you can turn Ortho mode on. Figure 3.7 shows some ellipses with the axes at various orientations.

As with circles, you cannot stretch ellipses. The aspect ratio set when the ellipse is first drawn persists. As with circles, if the entire ellipse is enclosed in the crosses/window box when using Stretch, it will be moved. If not, it is unchanged.

Curve

AutoSketch draws curves using the spline method. To draw a curve, you click the mouse at a number of control points. As you go, these points are joined by straight lines. When you finish the curve, a smooth curve is drawn, guided by, but not necessarily passing through, these points. You could think of each point as being like a magnet, pulling at a springy steel line. Each point pulls the curve towards it. You can make the line curve more strongly at a particular place by putting more control points near it.

The curve will always pass through the first and last points. It is possible for the curve to pass through other points. This is most likely to happen with gentle curves.

You normally complete a curve by clicking the last point twice. A closed curve can be created by making the first and last points the same. The curve is completed when you click the first point again, you do not need to double-click. Figure 3.8 shows some curves.

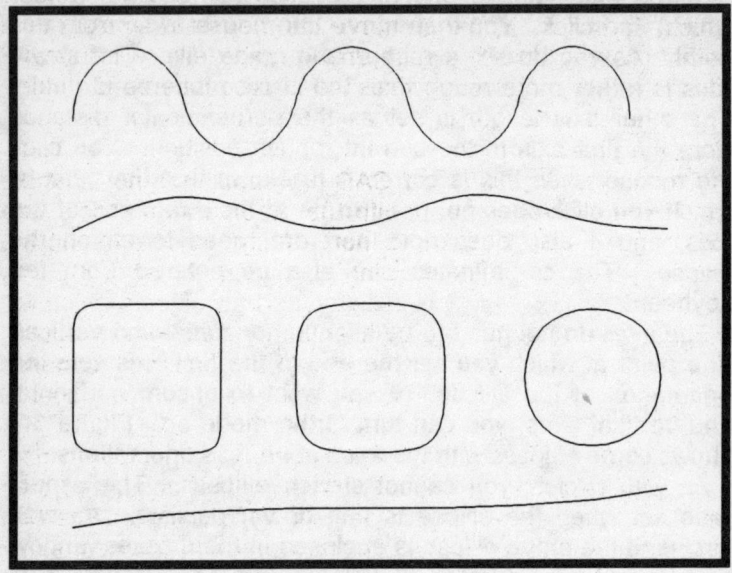

Figure 3.8. Open and closed curves.

The three closed curves in Figure 3.8 were drawn within square areas. The leftmost has five control points on each side, the two corners, halfway up each side, and two intermediate points, all equally spaced. The middle one has three control points per side, the corners and the halfway point. The rightmost has just the four corners as control points. This shows how adding points increases the 'pull' on the line.

The guide lines which appear between the control points normally are removed when the final curve is drawn. However, they can be left on the screen by setting Frame Mode on. To do this, display the Curve Settings dialog, either by double-clicking the Curve tool in the Draw toolbox, or by selecting Drawing Settings from the Utility toolbox, then clicking the Curve button. Having the frame visible may help you to understand the curve tool when first using it, and it may be useful when editing curves.

The other setting in the Curve Settings dialog controls the smoothness of the curve. Curves actually consist of small straight lines. By increasing the number of curve segments (from the default of 8), the curve can be made smoother. It will, however, take longer to draw and redraw. The size of drawing files containing curves will also be increased.

Pattern Filled Objects

With AutoSketch and most CAD programs, it is not possible to flood-fill objects drawn with the other drawing tools with patterns or colour, and it is not usually possible to fill the blank areas of the drawing between objects. With AutoSketch, however, it is possible to draw objects which will have a pattern fill. These objects can range from simple squares, rectangles and circles to polygons and complex shapes with a combination of straight and curved boundaries.

The pattern fill tool is rather like the polyline tool in use. Having selected it, you then click at the first point, and then at each corner, finishing the object by clicking on the first point again. At any point, you can switch to arc segments. As with polylines, if you want to start with an arc, you must turn on the Arc Mode tool before clicking the first point. As usual, co-ordinates can be entered from the keyboard.

There are 55 patterns supplied with AutoSketch, including blank and solid. It is possible to define your own patterns, but this is not a job for the faint hearted. If you want to try it, it is described in an appendix to the user's manual.

The pattern to be used is chosen using the Pattern Settings dialog. You can display this by double-clicking the Pattern Fill tool in the Draw toolbox, or by clicking the Drawing Settings tool in the utility toolbox and then clicking the pattern button. Samples of each pattern are displayed, and you can choose the one you want by double-clicking or making it active by single-clicking and then choosing OK. This dialog also allows you to change the size of the pattern with the Scale setting, and its angle.

You can also choose whether to have a boundary to your filled object. If Frame Mode is on and you choose to have a borderless filled object, the boundary will still be shown, but it will not print. Figure 3.9 shows some pattern filled shapes.

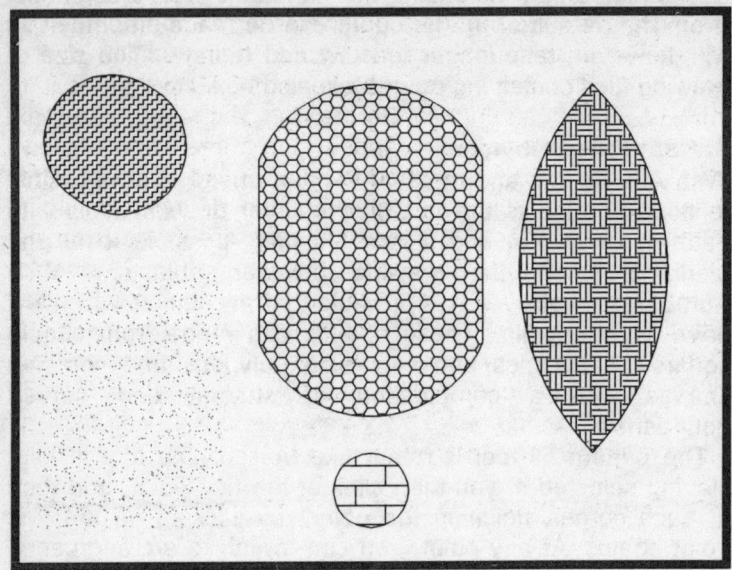

Figure 3.9. Some pattern-filled shapes.

Text
Text can be included in AutoSketch drawings for captioning or any other required purpose. In fact, substantial amounts of text may be included. Two methods of adding text are provided. Quick Text is for small amounts of text, such as single-line captions. The Text Editor is for larger amounts of minimally-formatted text, and also allows the importation of text (ASCII) from other programs.

Text can be displayed in a number of fonts supplied with AutoSketch. These include a number of letter styles, and also symbol fonts, including a music font. However, these are all stroke fonts. This means the letters are drawn with lines, and the results can be somewhat spidery in effect. This is generally satisfactory for technical drawings, but can be a problem for illustrations or display material. However, Release 2 of AutoSketch for Windows is capable of using

TrueType scalable fonts, as supplied with Microsoft Windows. This should allow substantially higher quality text than the stroke fonts.

As the available fonts are outline or stroke fonts, they can be altered in various ways, as well as being scaled over a wide range of sizes. (One old joke with CAD programs is to include a saucy limerick in the drawing, but to scale the text to such a small size that it appears as a line when printed.) The text can also be stretched to taller or wider aspect ratios than normal, or slanted to give oblique or italic (including reverse-italic) lettering. These changes are made from the Text Settings dialog. To display this, you can either double-click either of the text tools in the Draw toolbox, or click Drawing Settings in the Utility toolbox, and then click the Text button. This dialog also allows you to choose the font to be used. Figure 3.10 shows some text using AutoSketch fonts. TrueType fonts are very versatile, but do not allow as many effects as the stroke fonts.

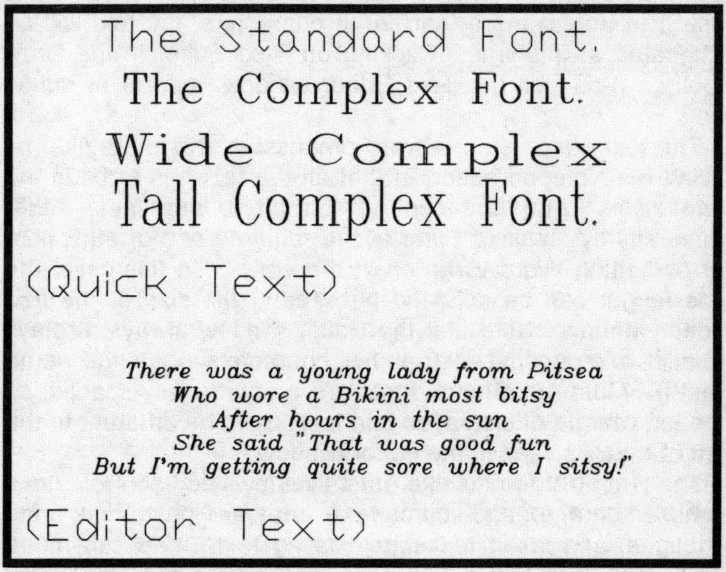

The Standard Font.
The Complex Font.
Wide Complex
Tall Complex Font.
(Quick Text)

There was a young lady from Pitsea
Who wore a Bikini most bitsy
After hours in the sun
She said "That was good fun
But I'm getting quite sore where I sitsy!"

(Editor Text)

Figure 3.10. Stroke-font text.

Quick Text

The Quick Text tool is for single lines of text. You can add additional lines below the first, but each line of text is a separate object for editing purposes. Each line may contain up to 256 characters.

To use the Quick Text tool, you first select it in the Draw toolbox or menu, and then click in the drawing where you want the text to display. You can then type in the text. Text entry is ended by pressing the Enter key.

If you want to add multiple lines of text, you should not press Enter. Instead, you should click the mouse anywhere on the drawing. Subsequent lines of text will be aligned below the first. Press Enter when you have added all the lines.

Text Editor

The Text Editor tool is used for adding substantial amounts of text. It also provides for text import. Up to 2048 characters can be entered using the text editor. If you try to use it to import more than 2048 characters, the text will be truncated at this limit. Clicking on Text Editor in the Draw toolbox produces the Text Editor window, a form of dialog box.

The text editor is not a word processor. It is more like the Windows Notepad editor, in that all the text has to be in the one style. The text can be formatted into lines, either manually by pressing Enter at the required end of each line, or by setting Word Wrap on in the editor. In this case, the line length can be adjusted by altering the size of the text editor window. Note that the Editor window always displays text in a monospaced font (all characters have the same width). Most AutoSketch fonts are proportionally-spaced, so the left margin of displayed text is likely to be different to the left margin as seen in the editor window.

The text editor works like most Windows edit controls (as it is based on one), and you can cut, copy and paste text, undo changes, and insert text into existing text. You can move the cursor with the mouse, and highlight text, in the usual way. You cannot insert tabs into the text, but it is possible to have the text aligned on the left or right margins, or centred.

Normally, you click at the point in the drawing where you want the text after clicking the text editor tool. This takes you into the text editor. When you have entered all the text, you click on OK. When you do this, the text is drawn on the screen. Normally, it will be drawn below the point where you clicked, to the right if you chose left justification, to the left if you chose right justification, or centred on this point if you chose centred justification. If you choose middle alignment, this controls the vertical positioning. The text will range equally above and below the selected point.

The text editor can also export text for use by other programs, or to be imported into other drawings. This could be useful for standard copyright or disclaimer notices.

4. PARTS AND ARRAYS

Parts and arrays are two ways of speeding up your CAD work. Parts allow you to save collections of objects from one drawing for use in other drawings. This is particularly useful for saving sets of symbols used in various professions. Arrays allow you to quickly draw objects arranged in regular linear, rectangular or circular patterns.

Parts

Nearly all CAD programs have some way of saving drawings in some format so that they can be quickly imported and used as components in new drawings. They may be called symbols, blocks or parts. In AutoSketch, the term parts is used.

The ability to save time by using libraries of parts is such that many symbol libraries are available from third-party suppliers. These include libraries of architectural symbols, symbols used in garden design, and electrical and electronic symbols. If commercial libraries are not available for what you require, or you have special requirements for style, you can draw your own libraries.

Many CAD programs have a special file format for blocks to allow rapid import. In AutoSketch, any standard drawing file can be used as a part, as the standard .SKD file format is used. However, it is worthwhile drawing up parts specially, so that you can be consistent in scale and setup. This allows you to build up drawings from parts without the joins showing.

Creating Re-usable Elements

Any drawing can be saved and used as a block. This includes drawings saved in the usual way, by selecting Save or Save As from the File menu. However, the File menu also has a Part Clip command. This has advantages for creating parts, as it allows selected objects (or groups) from a drawing to be selected and saved separately. It also allows a part base to be specified. This point will be at the cursor position when you are importing the part, making it easy to place it where required.

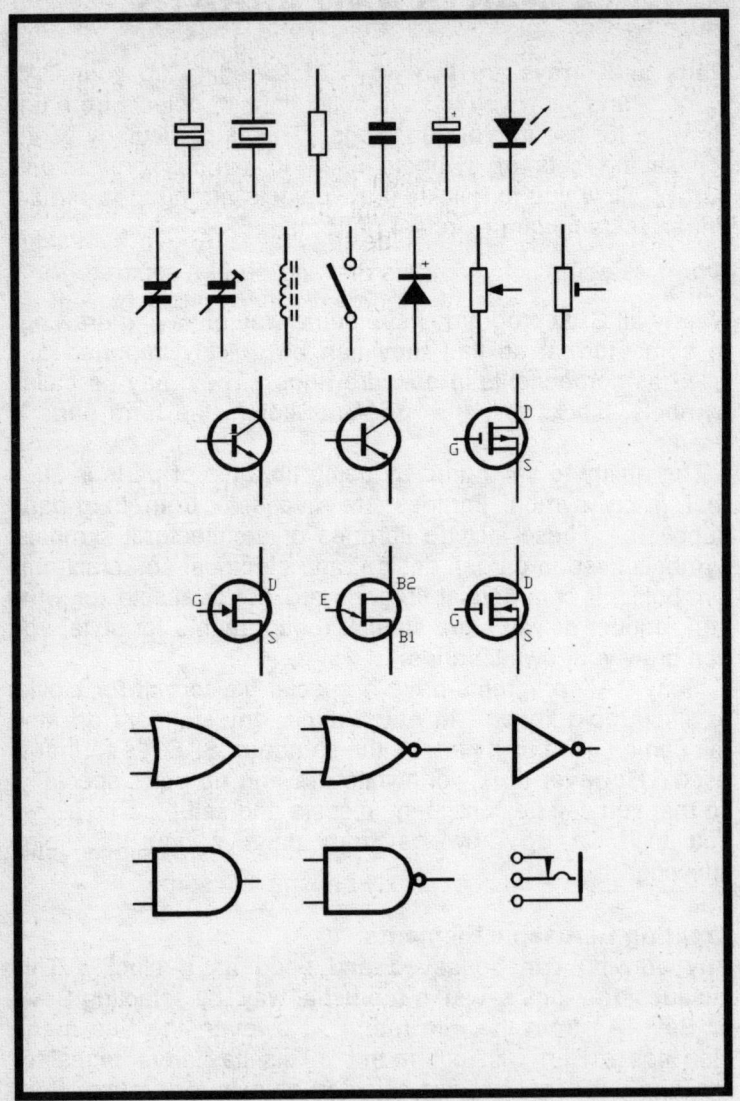

Figure 4.1. Electronic symbol library.

If you are creating a library of symbols, it can be advantageous to draw all the symbols together in one drawing, and then save them individually using Part Clip. There are several reasons for doing this. It allows you to be more consistent in style, as you can compare the symbols as you draw them. It allows you to be consistent in scale, as again you can compare each new element with what has gone before. You can also print out the drawing with all the symbols, and use it as a guide to what you have available. Finally, keeping copies of this drawing on file, separate from the computer, gives you a convenient, compact backup of something which may contain a great deal of work, and if one of your part files is accidentally altered or deleted, you can re-create it from this. Figure 4.1 is such a drawing, a library of electronics symbols.

When producing such a drawing, you should set up the page size, scale factors and grid and snap settings to what you will use for your drawings. This will simplify the part insertion process. You should also keep a note, mental or written, of such things as polyline widths and text sizes. This will make it easier to keep the original elements of drawings consistent with the imported parts, and, as stated above, stop the joins from showing.

It is a mistake to try to skimp on the number of parts you include in a library. If you need two symbols which have only a small difference, it is a temptation to only draw the one, with the intention of making the small alteration to it after importation when necessary. This is always a mistake. It is likely to require several operations of ungrouping and grouping again, and this quickly becomes irksome.

Saving Parts
Parts are saved using Part Clip on the File menu or toolbox. Though the Author normally prefers to have this as a menu, it can save time to switch to using the toolbox if several part clip operations are to be performed.

Before clipping each part. you will normally want to group the component objects. This will make it much easier to deal with the symbol as a unit when it is imported. You may want to group each symbol as it is finished, but this can result in a

63

lot of ungrouping and grouping again if you need to make alterations.

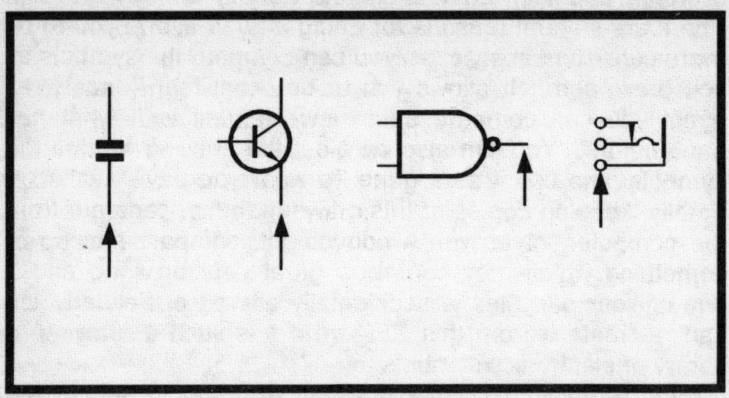

Figure 4.2. Some symbols with the part base indicated.

After choosing Part Clip, you are prompted first for the file name to be used for the part, and then for the Part Base. This is the point on the part which will be placed at the exact cursor position when the part is imported and being positioned. If the part will connect to the rest of the drawing, the part base should be a point at which the connection is likely to occur. Precise alignment can then be assured by using Attach or Snap when the part is placed. In these cases, it is also a good idea to use Attach when setting the part base.

If the part will not attach to the rest of the drawing, but will be a free standing element, it may be better to make the part base somewhere in the middle. This is likely to be true of some symbols used in architectural drawings, for example tables and chairs. Alternatively, you may find it more convenient to place the part base in the middle of the baseline, or in one corner. To some degree, it is a matter of personal preference, but it is usually a good idea to be consistent. In the electronic symbols in Figure 4.1, all the part bases are placed at the end of one of the wires. Figure 4.2 shows some of these with the part bases indicated.

Having set the part base, you then select the objects to be included in the part. If you have taken the advice to group all the object components of the part, this can be done simply by clicking again at the part base point, which will select the entire group. Otherwise, you must select each object separately, or use a crosses/window box. You complete the operation by clicking Part Clip again, or by choosing another drawing or editing tool. The part file is then saved.

When you use Part Clip, the files are saved in the directory AutoSketch recognises as the Parts directory. If you will be using several sets of parts, it may be advantageous to arrange them in further subdirectories off this subdirectory. If you want to do this, you must create the subdirectory you want to save the parts into before starting the clip operation. You can do this with File Manager or from DOS. It cannot be done from within AutoSketch.

Using Parts

Parts are imported using the Part tool which is in the Draw toolbox or menu. When you select this tool, a dialog appears. This is similar to the File Open dialog, in that it shows a small representation of each part on 'buttons'. You can select the part by double-clicking its button, or by clicking the button once, and then clicking OK. Figure 4.3 shows this dialog.

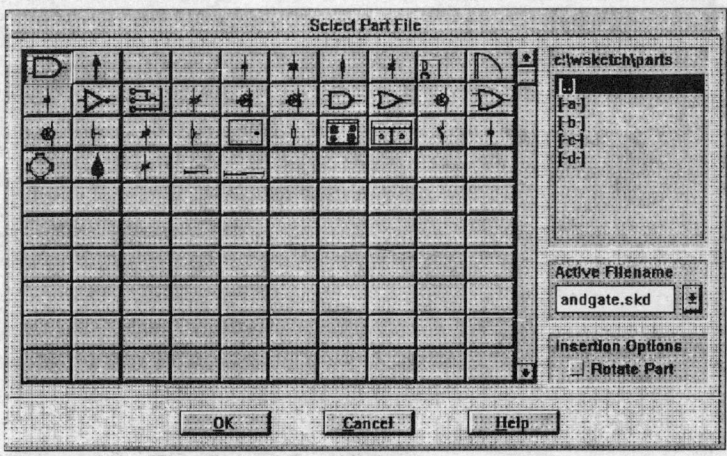

Figure 4.3. The Select Part dialog.

65

In this dialog is a check box labelled Rotate Part. If this is checked, it allows you to rotate the part before finally placing it in the drawing. It is important to make sure this check box is correctly set before closing the dialog. Though you can always rotate the part subsequently, using Rotate on the Edit menu, it is almost always easier to do it on insertion.

When you return to your drawing, the part will be displayed in dotted form, 'stuck' to the cursor at the position of the part base. If you are not rotating the part, it is simply a question of positioning the part where required, and clicking.

If the part is to be rotated, you must click anywhere in the drawing to establish a base point for the rotation. The rotation angle can then be set by moving the cursor with the mouse, or by entering the angle from the keyboard. The latter is often more convenient. The rotated part is then once again stuck to the cursor at the part base point, and can be positioned in the drawing by clicking at the required point.

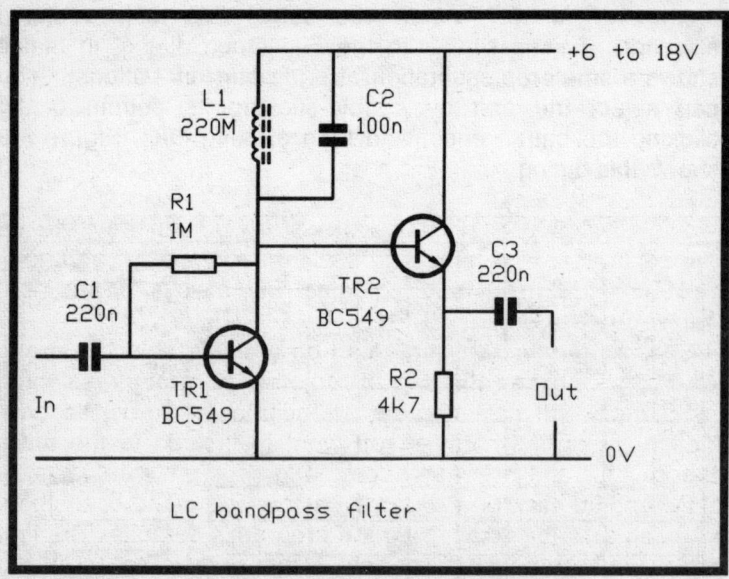

Figure 4.4. A circuit diagram drawn from parts.

No facility is provided to scale the part as it is imported. This can, of course, be done after it has been added to the drawing using Scale on the Edit menu. However, this is likely to involve moving the part as well, so it is a good idea to try to mach the scales of drawings and parts, as described above.

A part can be copied into a drawing any number of times, but if a large number of copies is required, it will be quicker to use Copy on the Edit menu after one copy has been imported, rather than to repeatedly use the Part File dialog.

Figure 4.4 is a circuit diagram drawn using some of the parts clipped from Figure 4.1.

Arrays

Arrays are used to make multiple copies of objects or groups of objects in a drawing. The copies must appear in a regular form, which can be linear, rectangular, or circular. Arrays are drawn by using Box Array (linear or rectangular) or Ring Array from the Edit menu or toolbox.

Box Array

Box Array creates multiple copies of objects in a rectangular pattern. The number and the spacings of the rows and columns can be individually adjusted, and either the rows or the columns (but not both) can be set to 1. In this way, linear arrays are possible.

The rows and columns in the array do not have to be horizontal and vertical. The baseline can be set at an angle. However, the rows and columns will always be at right angles to each other.

Each element in the array can be a single object, a group of objects, or a number of objects or groups selected individually. It can also be, or include, an imported part. You must draw whatever you want to include in the array before you select the Array command.

When you click on Box Array in the Edit menu or toolbox, you can draw an array using the program's defaults. The first thing you must do is to select the objects to form the elements of the array. If you are to include more than one object in the elements, they must be selected using a crosses/window box. It is normally preferable to group all the objects before starting the operation.

You must then set the column spacing. To do this, you click in the drawing to set a reference point, and then move the cursor to set the horizontal distance between columns. You may move the cursor left or right to set the spacing. It will not move vertically or diagonally. An outline of the object is shown as you move the cursor. The original object sets one corner of the array. The direction in which you move the cursor sets the direction in which the array will range from this point.

You then repeat this operation, but this time moving vertically to set the row spacing. Again, the direction in which you move the cursor sets the direction in which the array ranges. When this is set, the array is drawn, and you are presented with an Accept/Modify/Cancel dialog. By default, two rows and two columns are drawn. If the array is satisfactory, you click Accept. Cancel will erase the array and terminate the operation.

Clicking on Modify allows you to make changes to the array. When you set the column and row spacings, they are stored in the Box Array Settings dialog. This is displayed when you click Modify. From this dialog, you can change the number of rows, the number of columns, the spacing of either of these, and the baseline angle. You may alter any of these, but at least one of the rows and columns settings must be greater than one. When you click OK in this dialog, the array is redrawn (unless the program needs to prompt for new spacings), and you are presented with the Accept/Modify/Cancel dialog again. This cycle can be repeated as necessary, until the array is satisfactory.

As an alternative to setting actual row and/or column spacings, you may set the array to fit between two points. This is done from the Box Array Settings dialog. You can produce this on demand by double-clicking the box array tool or by selecting Drawing Settings in the Utilities toolbox and then clicking on the Box Array button. This dialog is shown in Figure 4.5.

There are two check boxes in this dialog headed Fit, one for rows and one for columns. If you check either or both of these, the row distance and the column distance indicated in this dialog will be used as the distance between the first and last rows and/or columns in the array, with the others equally spaced between them.

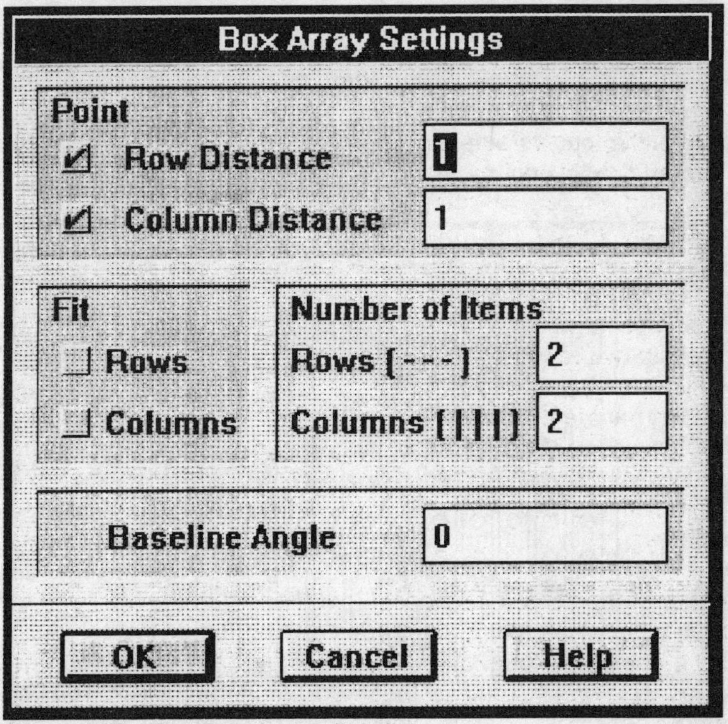

Box Array Settings

Point
- ☑ **Row Distance** `1`
- ☑ **Column Distance** `1`

Fit | **Number of Items**
- ☐ **Rows** | **Rows (- - -)** `2`
- ☐ **Columns** | **Columns [| | |]** `2`

Baseline Angle `0`

[OK]   [Cancel]   [Help]

Figure 4.5. The Box Array dialog.

Two check boxes labelled Point control whether you are prompted for row or column spacings. If these boxes are checked, you will be prompted to indicate the distance(s) with the cursor. If not, the distances in the associated text boxes are used. This applies both to setting column spacings and specifying a distance into which the array will fit. If distances for columns are positive, they will range right from the original element, if negative they will range left. If distances for rows are positive they will range downwards from the original element, if negative they will range up.

The number of rows and columns can also be preset here. They will remain in force until changed. In this way, you can set all the information needed to draw the array. This allows the drawing of arrays more precisely than could be done by using the cursor.

Finally, you can set the baseline angle. An angle of zero sets the baseline horizontal. Positive angles will rotate the baseline counter clockwise from this. Note that only the array is rotated. The elements will remain 'upright'. If you want to rotate the elements as well, draw the array and use Rotate on the Edit menu to rotate the whole thing.

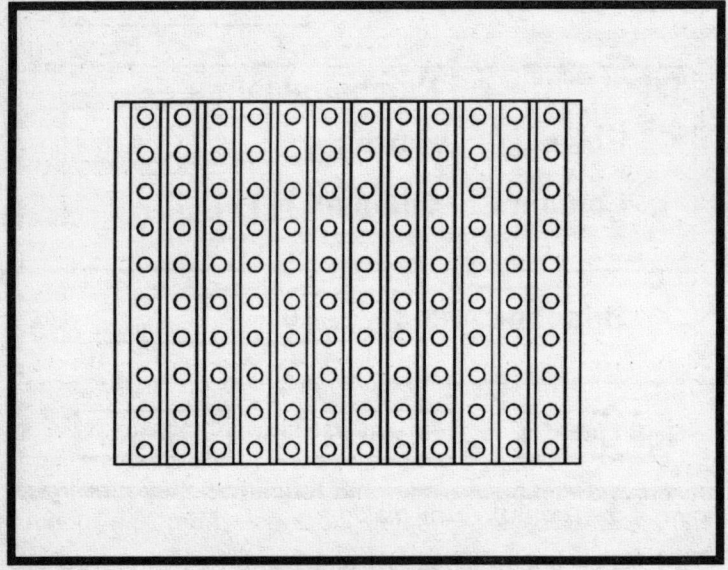

Figure 4.6. Drawing created with Box Array.

The elements of the array are individual elements. AutoSketch does not group them, but you can of course do this if necessary. If you want 'gaps' in your array, you can delete individual elements, or alter them in other ways.

You will see that the elements in the Box Array Settings dialog interact in several ways. This always tends to cause some confusion at first, but it is fun to experiment with arrays to get used to these controls. Figure 4.6 was drawn using box arrays.

Ring Arrays

Ring arrays are similar to box arrays in that they create copies of an original object or group of objects in a regular pattern, but this time they are placed in a circle or some part of it. The elements can be rotated around the centre point of the array as they are drawn.

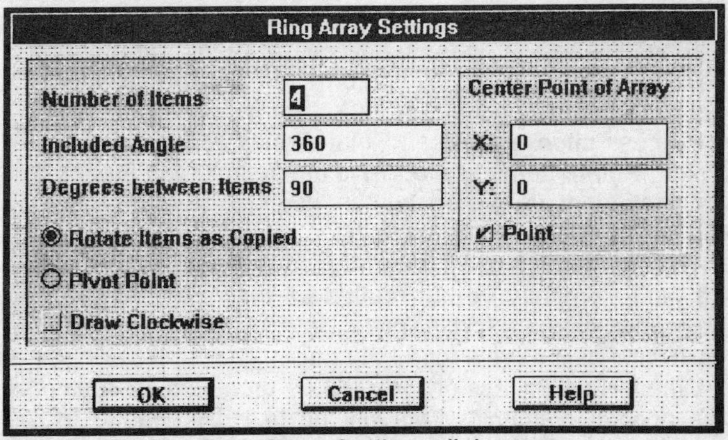

Figure 4.7. The Ring Array Settings dialog.

As with Box Array, you can use the defaults to draw an array simply. The defaults are to draw four elements, evenly spaced in a complete circle, and rotated as they are drawn. The array is drawn counter clockwise from the original element.

To draw a ring array, you click the Ring Array tool in the Edit toolbox, or select it from the menu. You must then select the objects to be included in each element. To select more than one object or group, use a crosses/window box. You will then be prompted to set the centre point of the array by clicking. The distance between this point and the original element sets the radius of the array. As with Box Array, you will be presented with an Accept/Modify/Cancel dialog.

The defaults can be changed from the Ring Array Settings dialog. This is produced by double-clicking on the Ring

71

Array tool or by selecting Drawing Settings from the Utilities menu, and then clicking the Ring Array button. This dialog is shown in Figure 4.7.

The Number of Items text box lets you set the total number of items in the array. This includes the original item.

The Included Angle box lets you set the part of the circle around which you want the elements to be placed. A setting of 360 will give a complete circle. 180 a semicircle, and so on. You cannot enter an angle setting greater than 360.

The Degrees between items box lets you set the spacing between the elements in the array. Obviously, these three settings interact. If you change one of them, the others will be altered if necessary to conform. Impossible settings will not be accepted.

You can choose between Rotate Items as Copied or Pivot Point. Rotate Items as Copied is the default, and means that each element is rotated by the appropriate angle as it is drawn, so that the elements 'radiate' from the centre point. If Pivot Point is turned on, this rotation is automatically turned off, and elements are not rotated as they are drawn, giving an effect like a bicycle pedal in normal use, remaining horizontal as it travels round the hub.

When Pivot Point is on, you will be prompted for a point in the original element. This will be like the bearing of the cycle pedal. This point will be kept equidistant from the centre of the array in each element.

Ring arrays are normally drawn counter clockwise. If you check the Draw Clockwise check box, arrays will be drawn clockwise.

The Centre Point of Array text boxes let you set the x and y co-ordinates of the array centre point. If the Point check box associated with these is checked, you will be prompted to set the centre point with the cursor.

As with box arrays, the elements in a ring array are not automatically grouped. They can be individually edited, and some deleted if required if you want an incomplete array.

The best way to fully understand all the Ring Array settings is again to practice with them. Figure 4.8 is a practice doodle with ring arrays.

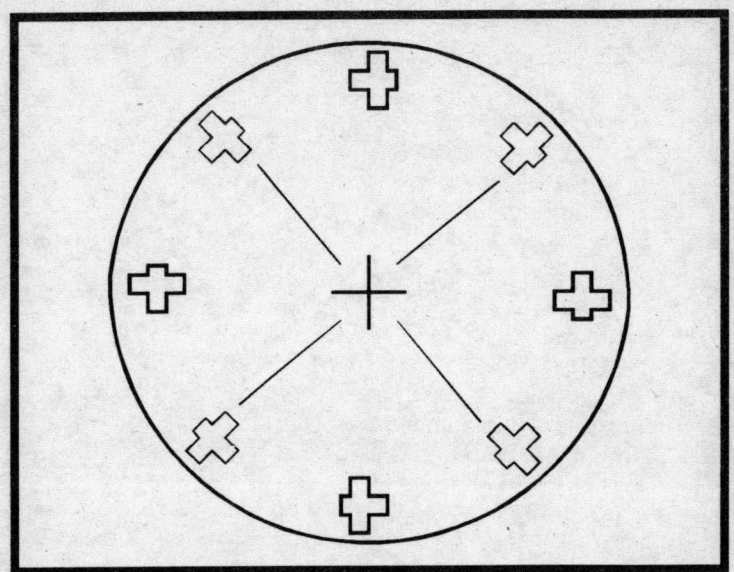

Figure 4.8. A Ring Array doodle.

5. CHANGING DRAWINGS

While drawings are work in progress, there will be many occasions when you will make small mistakes, or need to make small alterations. There are many facilities provided on the Edit menu for these purposes. There are also some things which can only be done by drawing objects and then applying editing procedures, especially where rotation is concerned. These facilities are described in this chapter.

Undo and Redo
There will be many occasions when a drawing operation will simply go wrong, and you would like to turn the clock back to before you started it. Undo will not let you recover the time, but it will allow you to return to an earlier stage in the drawing.

As you add each object to the drawing, a record of the operation is stored in a temporary file. This file is maintained throughout the drawing session. It is cleared each time you save your drawing. When you click on the Undo button (or use F2 on the keyboard), AutoSketch uses this file to determine the last operation, and undoes its effects. You can thus back up through the drawing to the point of the last save. Redo simply reverses the effect of the last Undo, so you can go backwards and forwards through a drawing.

How you use Undo depends to some extent on your purpose in using AutoSketch. For technical drawing, you may only use it to correct mistakes, in which case you may like to save your work frequently. Keeping the Undo file small speeds up operations. For more creative illustration and design work, where you may be working more experimentally, going back and forth through the drawing stages may be part of an experimental approach. In this case, you may need to be careful about when you save.

If you need to conserve disk space for any reason, Undo and Redo can be disabled from the Preferences tool. When this is done, the undo file is not created. This is particularly important with operations like creating arrays, as these use a lot of disk space for temporary files.

Move

If an object is originally drawn in what proves to simply be the wrong place, it can simply be moved. It is also possible to move several objects at once by using a crosses/window selection box to enclose them. Grouped objects will always move together.

Move is a simple tool to use. After selecting it, you select the object or objects to move. You then specify a reference point for moving the objects. This does not need to be a point actually on any of the objects. It can, in fact, be some distance from them. However, it will usually be a specific point, and it may be helpful to use Attach to find the point with precision.

You then specify a reference point to which the objects will be moved. The distance and direction by which the objects are moved is set by the displacement from the first reference point to the second reference point. As you move the cursor, an outline of the objects will move with it, and this can be used as a guide. However, if many or complex objects are involved, this will take some time to draw at each move, in which case it may not be much use. Waiting for redraws can be time consuming, but this is not necessary. You can move the cursor again without waiting for it to complete.

When the objects are where you want them, you click the mouse to redraw them in the new location. If this is unsatisfactory, you can use Undo to restore them to their original position.

Note that when moving objects, the setting of both the first and second reference points will be affected by the settings of any of Attach, Snap and Ortho which are active. It is always a good idea to check which, if any of these you have active before starting moves.

Copy and Multicopy

Copy is essentially similar to Move, but with the difference that the object(s) are left in their original location. Multicopy is much the same as Copy, but whereas Copy only allows one copy of the original to be made, Multicopy allows unlimited duplication.

With both Copy and Multicopy, you begin by selecting the object or objects to be copied. If more than one object is involved, you must use a crosses/window box to select them. Grouped objects will always be copied as a single object. You then specify a reference point for moving the copy or copies, following the same rules as for Move. For Copy, you then specify a single reference point for placing the copy, and the command terminates. For Multicopy, you can specify multiple points, placing a copy at each. The command terminates when you select another drawing or editing command.

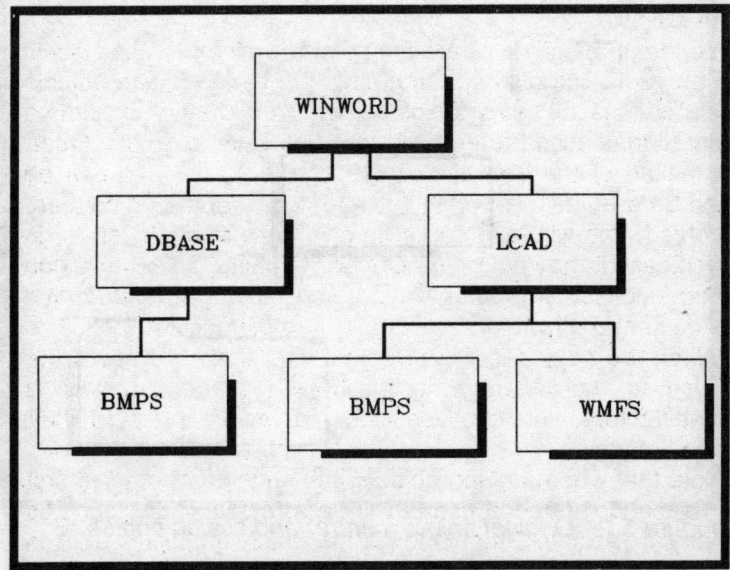

Figure 5.1. A block diagram created with Multicopy.

Multicopy can be useful in connection with importing parts. If several copies of a part are required, it is quicker to import one, and then use Multicopy on it to create as many as needed. This is especially true if the part needs to be rotated or scaled on import. Figure 5.1 used this method. The 'blocks' are a library part. One copy was imported and scaled, and five copies made. The text and lines were then added.

If you use Undo after Copy, the copy is removed. If you use it after Multicopy, all the copies are removed. In both cases, the original is left in place.

Scale
The Scale command lets you change the size of an object equally in vertical and horizontal directions. If you want to change the size of an object in one direction only, you need Stretch (see below).

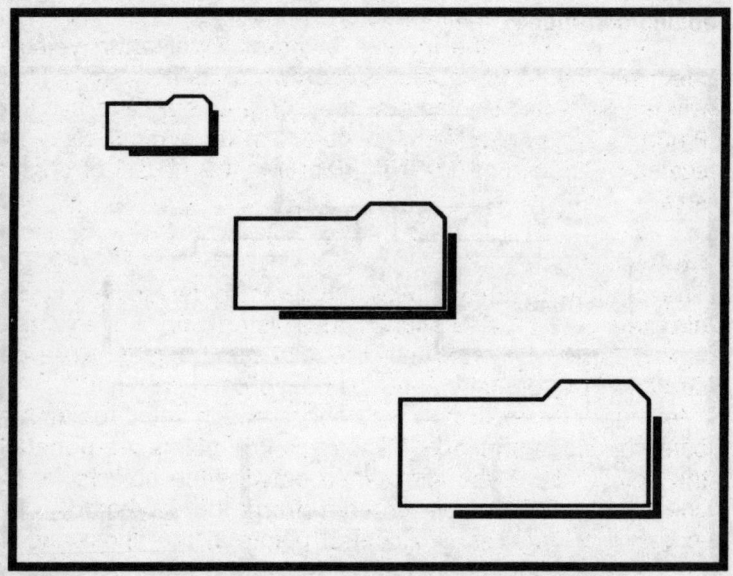

Figure 5.2. Original object (centre) and scaled copies.

Scale can work on multiple objects at once. As usual, grouped objects will be treated as one for scaling purposes.

After choosing the command, you select the object or objects you wish to scale. Single objects or groups can be selected by clicking. To select multiple objects, you must use a crosses/window box.

You must then specify a base point for the scaling operation. This base point determines the position of the scaled object. The distance from the object to the base point is also scaled. If you choose a base point 4 drawing units to the right of an object, and double the size of that object (a scale factor of 2), the scaled object will be placed 8 drawing units to the right of the base point.

Moving the cursor will set the scale factor. This is displayed in the prompt box. Values greater than one give an increase in size. Values less than one give a reduction in size. It can be difficult to get exact scaling factors with the cursor, but exact values can be typed in from the keyboard. This is a great improvement for the current version of AutoSketch over previous ones, which did not allow keyboard entry of scaling factors.

When you click the mouse, or press Enter after typing in the scale factor, the object is redrawn at its new size. Undo will restore scaled objects to their original size and position. Figure 5.2 shows a grouped object at its original size, and scaled by factors of 0.5 (half size) and 1.2 (120% of original size.

Stretch

The stretch command allows objects to be scaled in one direction only. It also allows other distortions. For example, boxes can be distorted into irregular quadrangles. You can stretch in any direction, not just horizontal or vertical.

When you use Stretch, you not so much select objects as control points on objects. These control points are generally the points where you click when drawing the objects, or the co-ordinate points you entered from the keyboard. For example, a line has two control points at the ends, and an arc has the control points at the two ends, and a point on the arc. A box has a control point at each corner.

You can select a single control point by clicking it (use of Attach recommended) or by drawing a crosses/window box enclosing only this one point. Multiple points can be selected by enclosing them in a crosses/window box. For stretch operations, the box always acts as a crosses box. Anything in the box is included.

Stretch is one command which effectively ignores grouping. Component objects in groups will be individually stretched, depending on whether or not they have control points selected.

Once your control points are selected, you pick a base point for the stretch. This does not need to be a point on the object, and in fact it can be better if it is not, so you can see the effect of the stretch clearly. You then move the cursor away from this point. The object(s) are stretched according to the direction and distance you move from the base point. You can also enter relative, polar or absolute co-ordinates from the keyboard. When the object is as you want it, you click the mouse, and it is redrawn in its new form.

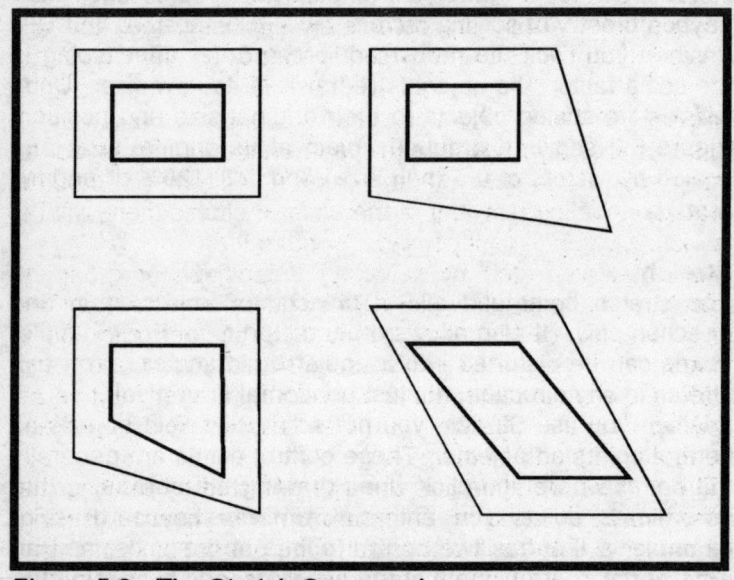

Figure 5.3. The Stretch Command.

The Stretch command is affected by Snap and Ortho. If Ortho is on, you will only be able to use the pointer to stretch objects in the vertical and horizontal directions. Undo restores stretched objects to their original shape.

Figure 5.3 shows the effects of the Stretch command. Top left is a figure consisting of two polylines, which have been grouped. At top right, one control point on the outer box was enclosed. At bottom left, one control point on the outer and one control point on the inner boxes were enclosed. At bottom right, two control points on each of the boxes were enclosed.

Not all objects can be stretched. In particular, circles and ellipses cannot be stretched. Circles will always remain truly circular, and ellipses will always retain the aspect ratio they were given when originally drawn. If the whole of these are enclosed by the crosses box, they will be moved. Otherwise, they will be unchanged.

Objects which can be stretched will only be changed in shape if not all of their control points are enclosed in the crosses box. If they are completely enclosed, they too will be moved, but will be unchanged in shape.

Rotate

This tool allows you to change the orientation of an object or group relative to the x and y axes. All objects can be rotated, including text, but in the case of circles there will be no visible effect except perhaps to move them.

As usual, you start by selecting the object, or group of objects, to be rotated. If you select several objects, they will all be rotated by the same amount. You then click on a centre of rotation. All objects will be rotated around this point, and remain the same distance from it after rotation as they were before. Rotate rotates and moves objects, unless the rotation point is at their centre.

The angle of rotation can then be selected by moving the cursor, or by entering the angle from the keyboard. If using the cursor, the angle is displayed in the prompt box. If Ortho is on, and you are using the cursor, you can only specify the angle in multiples of 90 degrees. Snap will also limit free movement of the cursor and interfere with specifying the angle. These restrictions do not apply to angles entered from the keyboard. You can also specify angles including fractions of degrees from the keyboard.

When the object is as you want it, you click the mouse to cause it to be redrawn in its new form. Undo will return all rotated objects to their original position and orientation.

Figure 5.4 shows the Rotate command. It shows two copies of a set of objects, as originally drawn, and rotated. The centre of rotation is indicated in the rotated copy by a cross. This is at the centre of one of the objects, which is not therefore moved. All the other objects were moved as well as rotated.

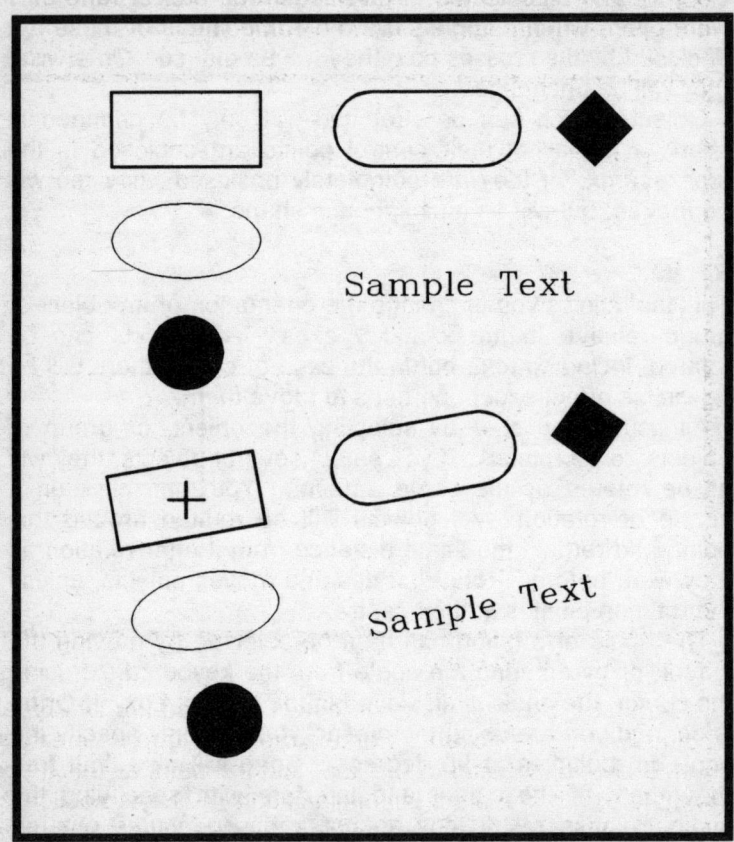

Figure 5.4. The effect of the Rotate Command.

Break
Break is used to trim lines or polylines, or to make gaps in lines, polylines or closed figures. The equivalent commands in some other CAD programs are trim or nibble. Break can also convert one object into two separate objects, without necessarily creating a visible gap between them.

Break can be used on all objects except pattern-filled objects. You cannot use Break on an object which is part of a group. You must use Ungroup first.

To use Break, you must first select the object. Only a single object may be selected. You will then be prompted to select a first break point and a second break point.

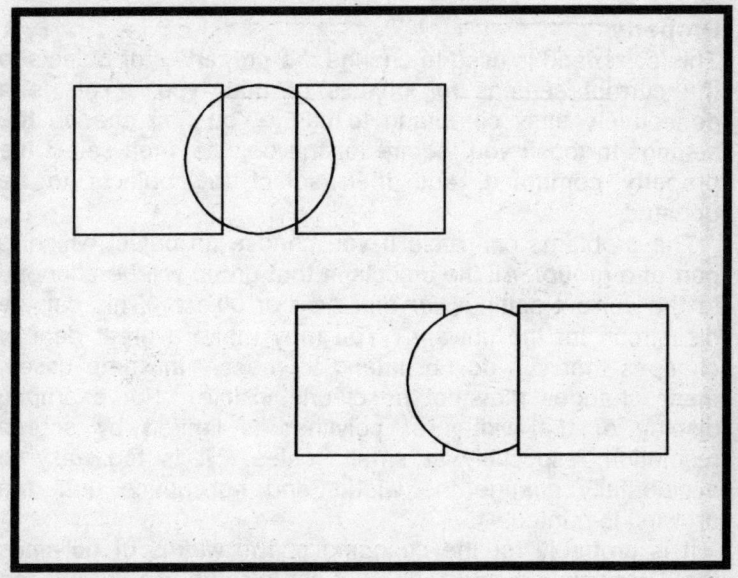

Figure 5.5. Using Break.

Generally, the section of the object between the two break points will be removed. For example, to trim a line, you would choose the end of the line, and the point at which you want to trim it (the order is not significant). This is applicable for all open objects, including arcs, curves, lines and open polylines. You can also cut a section out of any of these by choosing two points other than at the ends. You cannot, obviously, specify the same end for both break points.

With closed objects, which obviously have no end points, you will always be choosing two points within the object. The section which will be removed will be the section running counter clockwise from the first break point to the second break point. If you get the order wrong, click Undo and try again.

When you are trying to trim objects which intersect to remove the lines which overlap, Attach can be very useful to find the intersection points. Figure 5.5 shows what can be done with this.

Property

This command is used to change the properties of objects to the current settings for objects of that type. This is a deceptively easy command to use. You first change the settings to those you require for the objects, then select the property command, and then select the objects to be updated.

The problems can arise if you choose an object which is part of a group. All the objects in that group will be changed to the current settings *for that type of object.* This can be disastrous for the unwary. You may make a great deal of changes that you do not intend to make. In some cases, these changes may not be clearly visible. For example, display of the widths of polylines is limited by screen resolution, especially at small scales. It is too easy to accidentally change the widths and not notice until the drawing is printed.

It is probably for the changing of the widths of polylines that Property is most used, but it can also be used to change text size and style, and the pattern used in filled objects. It is a very useful command, but be careful if you are using grouped objects.

6. DRAWING ASSISTANCE

In CAD programs, points in drawings are stored to high precision, and it is possible to draw at a small scale (i.e. small on the screen) and then print at a much larger scale. The precision at which it is possible to work may become a problem, as small inaccuracies of placement when drawing may be quite noticeable errors in printed drawings.

Trying to remember, or having to note down, the co-ordinates of all the points in a complex drawing would rather defeat the point of CAD, so various ways are provided of ensuring accuracy when separate objects in a drawing must have common points. Ironically, these mostly work by limiting the free movement of the cursor.

It should be noted that all the facilities described in this chapter apply only to drawing with a pointing device, such as a mouse or graphics tablet. You can always enter any co-ordinates or angles from the keyboard.

Snap
The effect of Snap is indeed quite simply to limit the free movement of the cursor. When Snap is on, you actually have two cursors. The normal arrow or hand cursor moves normally, but there is also a small cross-hair cursor. This will only move to fixed positions at regular intervals across and down the screen. The setting of these points has been described in Chapter 2. The intervals between points in the two directions do not need to be equal, though they nearly always will be. The grid can be made equal to the snap intervals, and displayed if you need to see where the snap points are.

Snap is often most useful in the early stages of a drawing, when the main elements are being created. It enables truly rectangular figures to be drawn quickly, and sets of circles to be made truly concentric when required. Since Snap is set in drawing units, thoughtful settings, appropriate to what you are working on, will simplify drawing 'real world' objects to correct sizes.

You can change the snap settings at any time while drawing, and this may be necessary when changing the scale at which you are working. However, this can prevent you from moving the cursor to previous points in the drawing, if these do not fall on snap points at the new setting. You can, of course, temporarily turn Snap off if this is a problem. It can be turned on and off at any time. It is perfectly legitimate to set one end of a line with Snap on, then turn it off before setting the other end. You may turn it on and off many times in drawing a Polyline.

Attach

When you are well into a drawing, and most of the main objects have already been drawn, Snap becomes of less use. This is especially true if you have done much editing, especially using Rotate, or if you have been importing parts drawn without Snap, or using different settings. Snap will not be a lot of help in these cases.

Attach is a tool which is specifically for finding existing points in a drawing. It can find such things as the centres of circles and ellipses, the ends of lines, node points on polylines, and the points at which lines intersect. How to set the Attach settings is described in Chapter 2, together with a list of the eight attach modes.

Attach is particularly useful with editing operations such as Break. If you need to use Break to trim a line to the point where it crosses another line, you can set Attach to find ends of lines and intersect points. One of these will be your first break point, and the other the second.

The ability to use Attach to find intersect points is very important. Where circles and diagonal lines are involved, intersect points will very frequently not fall on snap positions, even if all objects have been drawn using Snap. Attach is the only way to find these points with exact precision.

Attach does have some pitfalls for the unwary. If you experience strange occurrences, such as positioning an inserted part, and having it drawn some distance from where you clicked, Attach may be the culprit. If you have Attach set to find the midpoint and end points of lines, and you click on a line to join the part to it, Attach will alter the insertion point to an end or the exact middle, depending on which is nearer to where you clicked. Similarly, if Centre mode is on, and you click on a circle, you will snap to the centre of the circle.

To use Attach effectively, you do need to know whether it is on or off, and to keep track of which modes are in force. It can affect many operations, including editing operations like Scale, Break and Rotate, and also the measuring tools, as well as the drawing tools. Like Snap, it can be turned on and off in the middle of operations as and when necessary.

A difference between Snap and Attach is that Snap will always move to a snap point, whereas Attach will only snap to an attach point if it can find one. If it cannot, where you click is where you get.

Ortho

The effect of the Ortho tool is to constrain lines drawn with it to exactly vertical and horizontal directions. It also similarly affects other drawing and editing tools.

Ortho is useful when you want complete freedom in selecting points, but you want to maintain exactly horizontal and vertical lines. Using the grid can also help keep lines horizontal and vertical, but restricts placement. With Ortho, you can position the first point anywhere, but then, as you move the cursor, the rubberband line will always be aligned with either the x or the y axis, depending on the direction in which you move the cursor.

The circuit diagram in Figure 4.4 was drawn partly using Ortho. Though the main lines were drawn using the grid, some of them, such as the line from TR2 to TR1, were not on the grid. Ortho made it easy to keep this line horizontal. Ortho also limits rotation of objects to intervals of 90 degrees. This was useful for the rotated components C1, R1, and C3.

If you want to use Ortho to draw a line precisely from a point to join exactly onto another line, the best way is to use Attach to find the point, draw the new line slightly past the existing line, and then use Break and Attach (to find the intersection) to trim off the excess.

Ortho will probably be used less than most of the other aids by most users, but when needed it is invaluable. It sounds limited, but in fact it is flexible and versatile. You might say it is a acquired taste.

Frame

This tool is only applicable to spline curves. It consists of a series of straight lines, and is only displayed if Frame mode is on (set from the View menu or toolbox).

Though you can edit curves with the frame either on or off, it is often easier with frame on. Curves can be altered by using Stretch on the control points. The frame is necessary to allow the control points to be located.

When breaking a curve, the effects can be unpredictable, as all the control points will remain. It can be better to break the frame instead. This will also break the curve, but the effect is much easier to predict.

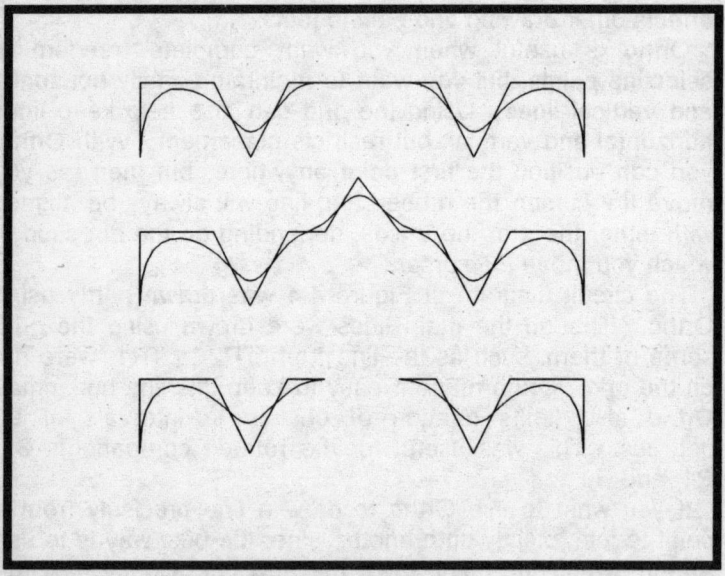

Figure 6.1. Curves with frame mode on.

Figure 6.1 shows curves complete with frames. The original curve is at the top. The middle curve shows the effect of Stretch on one of the control points. The bottom curve shows the effect of breaking the frame.

There is an interesting point concerning this diagram. When Frame mode is on, the frame should be shown on screen only, but not in any printed output. This figure is not a screen dump. It is included in the word processor document (producing camera-ready copy) using Object Linking and Embedding (OLE). The frame is shown. This is very useful here, but probably a mistake. Figure 6.2 shows the curves with the frames off.

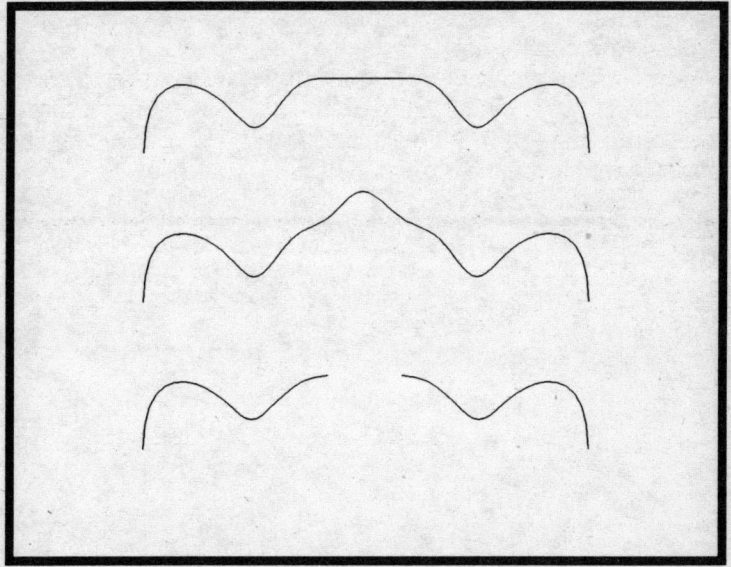

Figure 6.2. As Figure 6.1 but without frames.

7. MEASUREMENTS

On technical drawings, it will frequently be required to display measurements of objects in the drawings. Most CAD programs have some means of calculating and displaying measurements. AutoSketch can display horizontal, vertical, and angle dimensions, and can also display the distance between two points, at any angle.

Besides these four displayable measurements (which is to say, within the drawing), AutoSketch can also measure angles, areas, distances, bearings, and co-ordinates at a point. These are displayed in a message box, but not included in the drawing unless you add them yourself.

All these items are in the Measure menu or toolbox. This also includes the Show Properties option which will display the properties of any selected object. This will not be further discussed here.

One point about linear dimensions is that they are always displayed (in drawings or otherwise) in terms of drawing units. The Area measure tool displays 'square drawing units' in the dialog. When you include dimensions in drawings, you need to put somewhere in the drawing a statement like 'all dimensions in inches/metres/millimetres', or whatever you decide a drawing unit represents.

Horizontal Dimension
This tool allows you to draw a dimension which shows the horizontal distance between two points, ignoring any vertical displacement of the points. It will thus only show the length of a line between the two points (real or imaginary) if the two points have the same vertical co-ordinate.

To use the tool, you click the Horiz. Dimension tool in the Measure toolbox, or select it from the menu. You then click the first point. Attach or Snap may be useful here in obtaining exact dimensions. You then click the second point.

The next operation is to set the Dimension line location. This is where the dimension line will be drawn. This line is always drawn horizontally, regardless of the bearing of a line between the two selected points. You may click at any point along the horizontal line where you want the dimension to be drawn.

AutoSketch draws two vertical extension lines to the place where you want the dimension line, and it draws the dimension line, a straight line with arrows at the ends, between them. The dimension text is written above the line. If the text does not appear, it may be that it is too small, or vastly too big. The text size can be changed if necessary with the Property tool on the Edit menu.

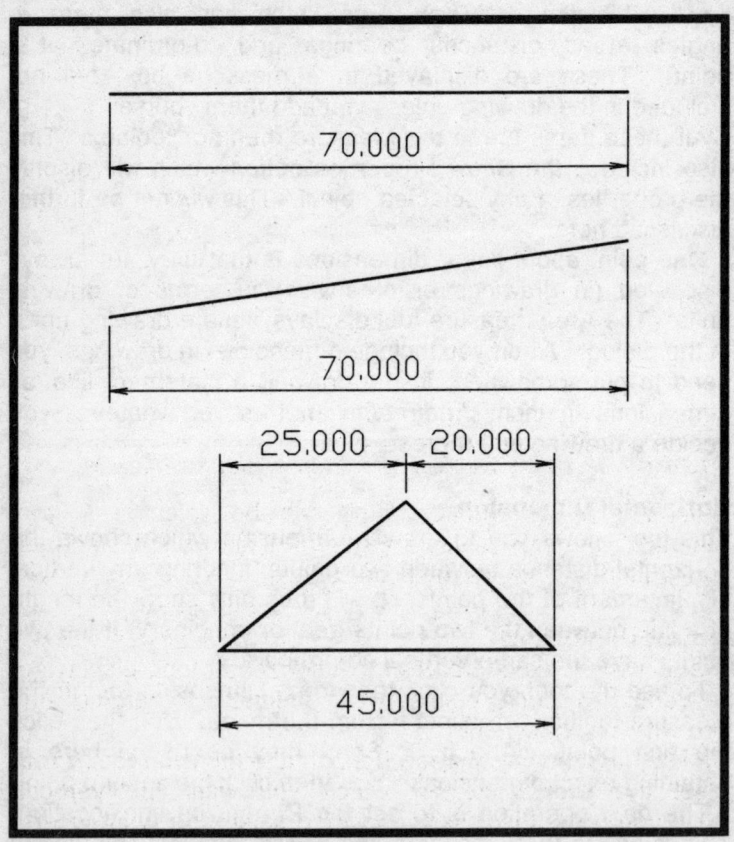

Figure 7.1. Horizontal Dimensions.

Figure 7.1 shows some objects with horizontal dimensions indicated.

In the Dimension Settings dialog there is an Offset with Leader option. This allows you to place the dimension text away from the dimension line. When this is checked, after selecting the two points, you will be prompted to create the leader, and then to indicate the point at which you want the text. Figure 7.2 shows a triangle with a dimension with an offset and leader.

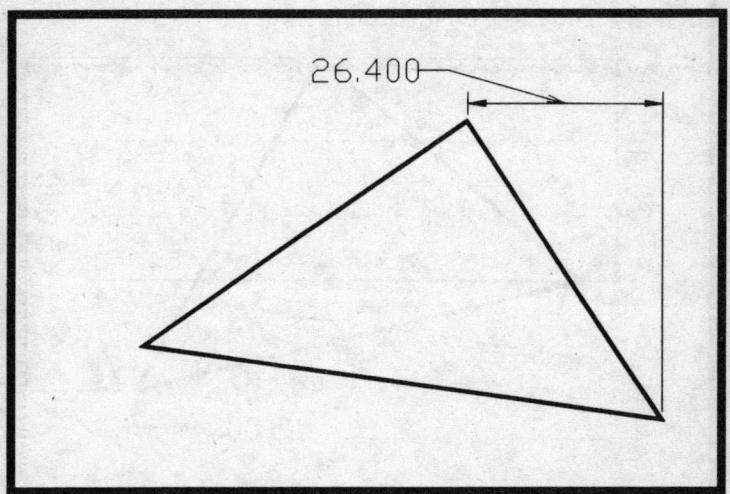

Figure 7.2. A figure with an offset dimension with leader.

A number of arrowhead styles can be selected in the Dimension Settings dialog. Figure 7.1 shows the standard type. Figure 7.2 shows the solid style.

Vertical Dimension
This tool is the counterpart of the horizontal tool, displaying the vertical distance between two points, disregarding any horizontal displacement.

In use, it is exactly like the horizontal dimension tool. You select the two points for which you want the vertical separation to be displayed, and then select the point where you want the dimension line to be drawn. The dimension text is drawn to the left of this line, and is rotated so that it reads from bottom to top.

93

As with Horizontal Dimension, it is possible to have the dimension text offset from the dimension line, with a leader. Figure 7.3 shows some vertical dimensions, including an offset one. Note that when an offset and leader is used, the text is drawn normally (horizontally).

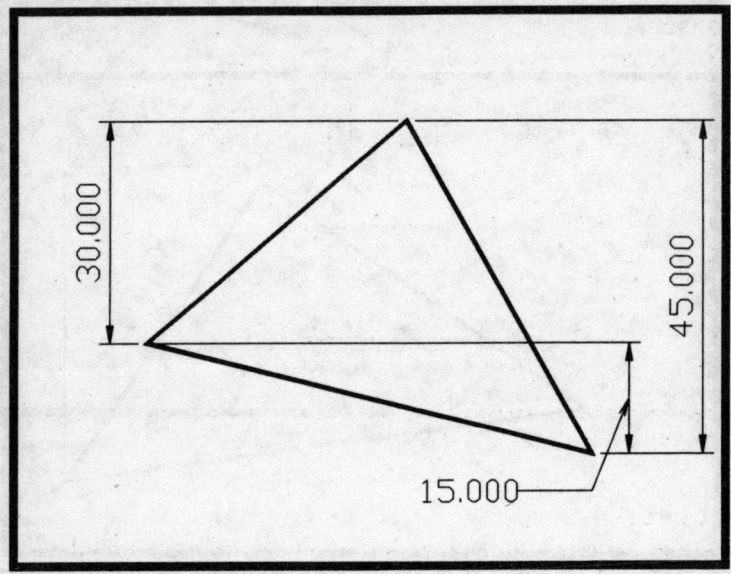

Figure 7.3. Vertical dimensions.

Align Dimension

Align Dimension is used to display the distance in a straight line between two points, at any angle. The two points do not need to be connected by a line, or to be on the same object.

Again, this command is just like the previous two to use. You select the two points, and the position of the dimension line. This is drawn parallel to the line between the two points. The text is drawn above the dimension line, rotated to the same angle. As with Vertical Dimension, if you use an offset with leader, the text is drawn horizontally. An example of this is shown in Figure 7.4.

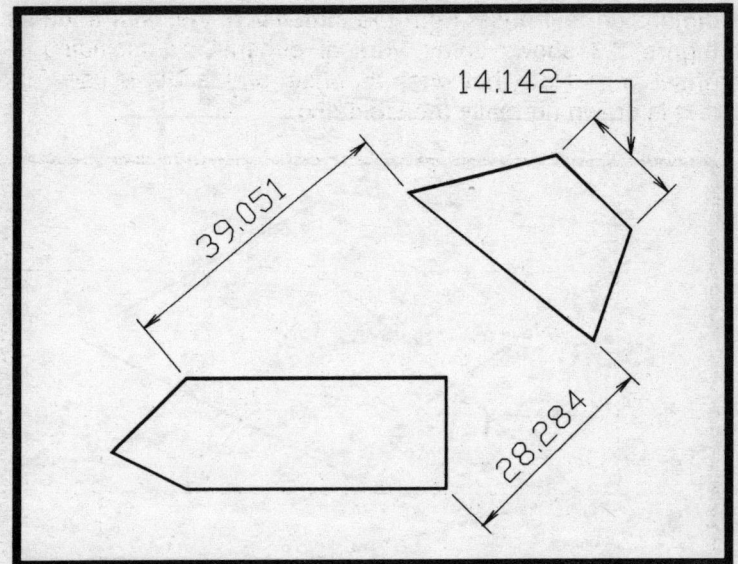

Figure 7.4. Align dimensions.

Angle Dimension
Angle Dimension displays the angle between two lines. The lines must be non-parallel, but they do not need to intersect. An angle dimension consists of an arc, with the text at a break in the arc. The arc is always less than 180 degrees.

To draw an angle dimension, you will be prompted to select the first line, and then the second line. You may select the lines anywhere along their length. You will then be prompted to select the location of the dimension line arc. If you choose a location where the space between the lines is too small for the dimension arc, arrow and text to fit, a dialog will appear prompting you for a new location.

With very small angles, the arrows are drawn outside the lines, with the text within the angle. If there is insufficient room for the text, you will be prompted for a location outside the angle. The offset and leader line facility is not available for angle dimensions. Figure 7.5 shows some angle dimensions.

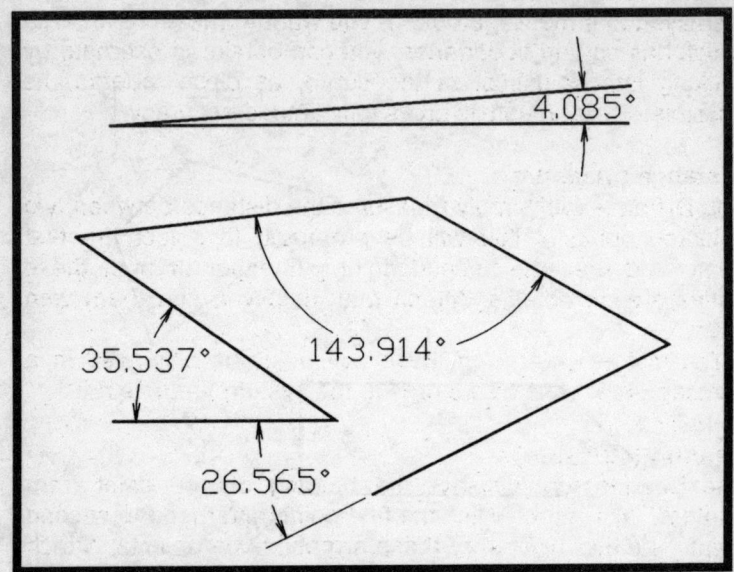

Figure 7.5. Some angle dimensions.

The remaining measure commands measure various aspects of a drawing, and display the results in a message box. They cannot, however, automatically include the results in the drawing.

Angle (measure)
The Angle tool measures the angle formed by three points, rather than the angle between two lines. You will be prompted for the base point, the first direction, and the second direction. The result is displayed in a message box. This displayed angle is stored in the system variable /langle.

Area (measure)
The Area tool measures the area within a polygonal perimeter. After you choose this tool, you will be prompted for the first point on the perimeter, and then for each further point, until you close the figure by clicking the starting point again. You can use Snap or Attach to help find this point.

Both the enclosed area and the length of the perimeter are displayed in a message box. If you want to measure an area which has curved boundaries, you can obtain an estimate by clicking lots of points on the curve, as close together as possible. This obviously gives only limited accuracy.

Distance (measure)

The Distance tool simply measures the distance between two selected points. You will be prompted to select the first point, and then the second point. If either or both these points are on objects, Attach may help you find them with precision.

The distance between these two points is displayed in a message box. It is also stored in the system variable /ldist.

Bearing (measure)

The Bearing tool displays the bearing of one point from another. You simply click the first point, and then the second point. If either or both of these are points on objects, Attach may help to find them. The bearing is measured counter clockwise from the first point to the second. The angle is displayed in a message box, and also stored in the system variable /langle.

Point (measure)

The Point tool displays the co-ordinates of a point. You simply click the point required, and the co-ordinates are displayed in a message box. This can be useful if you want to use the grid and/or snap features, and are unsure of the current scale at which you are working. Use Point to find the co-ordinates of one point, then move away from it by the grid spacing you would like to use, and find the co-ordinates of this point. Use the difference between them as your grid setting.

8. PRINTING

It is at the stage of printing a drawing that the relationship between drawing units and real world units is set. This is part of determining the size at which your drawing will be printed on the page.

Figure 8.1 shows the Print Settings dialog. It is here that sizing the drawing to fit the page is done. To do this, you need to know how big your drawing is in terms of drawing units. You may know this already, if you have drawn to a specific scale, but if you have been working freely, without much reference to co-ordinates, you may need to measure your drawing. You can use the Distance tool in the Measure toolbox for this.

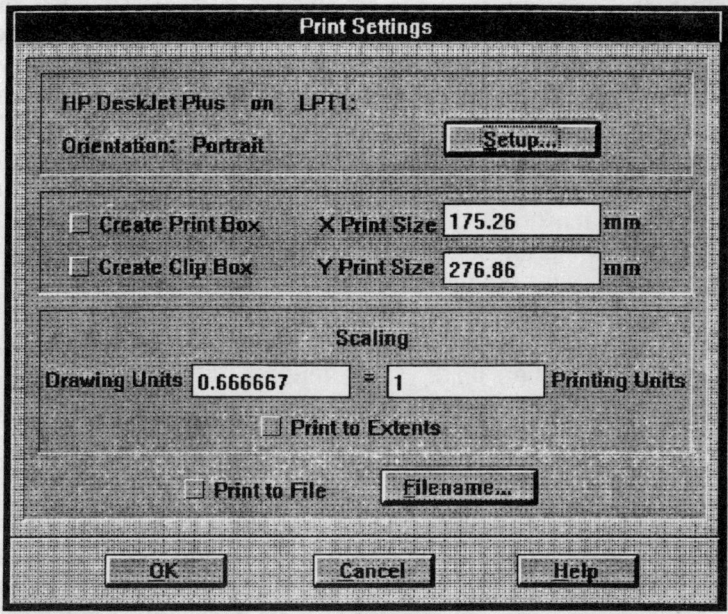

Figure 8.1. The Print Settings dialog.

You determine the size by setting the ratio of drawing units to printing units. The printing units will be either inches or millimetres. The units in use will be displayed beside the X

Print Size and Y Print Size text boxes in the Print Settings dialog. The default sizes shown in these boxes are the maxima which the selected printer can print. You can alter these to smaller or larger values, but in the latter case, the program will refuse to print.

If you simply want to print your drawing as large as possible, you can check the Print to Extents box in the Scaling section of this dialog. The scaling will then be calculated for you.

If you want to print to an exact scale, you need to work out the ratio of drawing units to printer units. You can make this easy for yourself, if you want to print drawings of objects at life-size, by using one drawing unit to represent one printing unit. For example, the drawing of a 5.25 inch disk (Figure 2.8) was drawn with one drawing unit representing 1 inch. With the printing units set to inches, it is just a case of setting one drawing unit to one printing unit, and the disk prints exactly life-size.

With such things as Architectural drawings, it will not be possible to print them life-size, for obvious reasons. Engineering drawings may need to be smaller or larger than life size. If you need to work at a 1 inch to 1 foot scale, you can use each drawing unit to represent 1 foot. If you then set 12 drawing units to 1 printing unit, you will achieve your scale. If you produced an engineering drawing with 1 drawing unit representing 1 millimetre, and you needed the drawing to be ten times life size, you would set 1 drawing unit to 10 printing units. The general rule is that drawing units larger than printing units will enlarge the drawing, printing units larger than drawing units will reduce it.

To be able to print, you must have a print box on your drawing. This is created, using the Print Settings dialog, simply by checking the Create Print Box check box. The print box is created and added to your drawing when you click OK in this dialog. If you cannot see this box when you return to your drawing, click the Zoom Full tool. Figure 8.2 shows a drawing with a print box.

The print box allows you to see the size and position of your drawing on the page. If the size is not satisfactory, you can go back to the Print Settings dialog and produce another print box at a different scale setting. You can have several print boxes in a drawing, but only one must be visible when you start the printing operation. They can be erased like a drawing object if required.

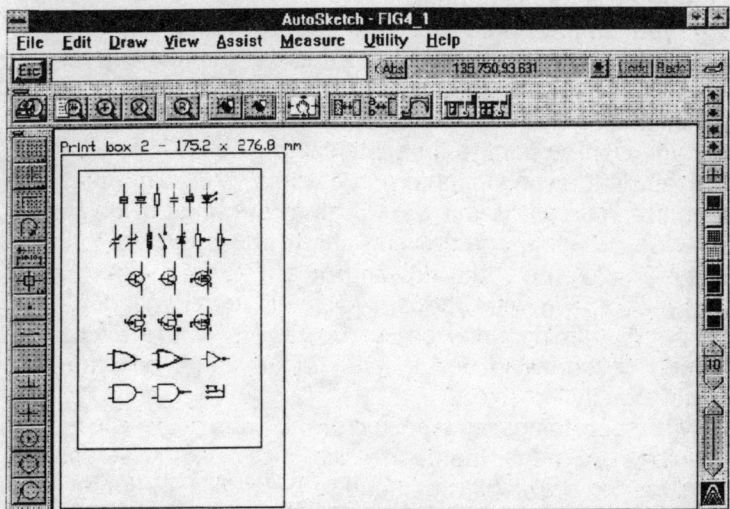

Figure 8.2. A Drawing with a Print Box.

The orientation of the paper can be either Landscape (long side horizontal) or Portrait (long side vertical). If you need to change from one to another, you can do this from the Print Settings dialog by clicking the Setup button. This produces the Windows Printer Setup dialog.

The positioning of the drawing on the paper can be altered by moving the print box. This is done using Move on the Edit menu. The print box can be selected like any drawn object, and dragged so that the drawing is at the required place on the page. However, note that the print box represents the printable area of the page, not the entire sheet. The margins may not be even, so centring the drawing in the print box may not exactly centre it on the page. A few tests will show you if any offset is necessary for your printer.

INDEX